FREEDOM'S HOLY LIGHT

FREEDOM'S
HOLY
LIGHT

by Richard H. Schneider

Guideposts

CARMEL • NEW YORK 10512

Published in Nashville, Tennessee, by Thomas Nelson, Inc. and distributed in Canada by Lawson Falle, Ltd., Cambridge, Ontario.

Printed in the United States of America.

Unless otherwise noted, the Bible version used is THE NEW KING JAMES VERSION. Copyright © 1979, 1980, 1982, Thomas Nelson, Inc., Publishers.

This Guideposts edition is published by special arrangement with Thomas Nelson Publishers.

Library of Congress Cataloging-in-Publication Data
Schneider, Richard H., 1922—
    Freedom's Holy Light.

    1. Statue of Liberty (New York, N.Y.)–History. 2. Bartholdi, Frédéric Auguste, 1834–1904. 3. Liberty. 4. New York (N.Y.)–Buildings, structures, etc.
I. Title.
F128.64.L6S36   1985   974.7'1   85-18936

DEDICATION

AMERICA'S ONE-WOMAN WELCOMING COMMITTEE

Measurements

- Her height from heel to head: 111 feet, 1 inch. About the height of an 11-story building.
- Her right arm is 42 feet long, measuring 12 feet around at its greatest thickness.
- Her right hand measures 16 feet, 5 inches in length.
- Her index finger extends 8 feet, almost 2 feet longer than the average bed.
- A fingernail covers almost 1 square foot (13 by 10 inches).
- Her waist measurement is 35 feet.
- Miss Liberty's head is 10 feet wide and measures 17 feet, 3 inches from chin to top.
- Each eye is 2$\frac{1}{2}$ feet wide.
- Her nose is 4$\frac{1}{2}$ feet long.
- Her mouth is 1 yard wide.
- Miss Liberty weighs 225 tons, consisting of 100 tons of copper sheathing and 125 tons of steel framework.
- Her crown has 25 windows. Forty people can stand within it at once.
- She holds a tablet that is 23 feet, 7 inches long, 13 feet, 7 inches wide, and 2 feet thick. It is emblazoned *July 4, 1776* in roman numerals.
- Miss Liberty stands on a granite pedestal that is 89 feet tall. It, in turn, rests on a foundation that is 65 feet high.
- Overall, the height of the Statue of Liberty from base of the foundation to her torch is 305 feet, 1 inch, which is about the same as a 30-story building.

CONTENTS

In Appreciation To

my wife, Betty, who typed, encouraged,
and suggested the title, "Freedom's Holy Light";

her father, Rolla Renfro, who instilled in me
an appreciation of history;

the staff of the Rye Free Reading Room,
Rye, New York, who were so helpful in
supplying reference information;

Donna Mayfield of Arlington, Virginia, who
researched historical photos; and

Brooks Gibson of New York City, who researched recent photographs.

9

I want to thank Dick Schneider for asking me to contribute a few words to his book on the Statue of Liberty. Works like this can only increase our reverence for liberty, for the God who bestows it, and for the sacrifices so many have made for it.

I've often thought that God put this land of ours where He did to be found by a special kind of people—those who love liberty enough and have courage enough to make any sacrifice, even to leave home, to secure it; those who dare to live the motto, "Where liberty dwells, there is my country."

Millions of quiet heroes and heroines the world over have sought a new and better life in this land of liberty and opportunity. Many of them, including my own great-grandparents Michael and Catherine, arrived here before there was a Statue of Liberty. Their beacon and their reward was liberty itself. One hundred years ago, though, their ideal of liberty was given dramatic and timeless personification in Frédéric Auguste Bartholdi's statue.

We are forever indebted to Bartholdi and to all those in France and in America who made possible this beloved image of liberty. Today, we congratulate everyone taking part in a similar voluntary effort to restore the Statue of Liberty and Ellis Island, where so many entered our country for the first time.

God willing, the Statue of Liberty will always call out to freedom-lovers here and around the world. I'm thinking of people like the sixty-five Vietnamese refugees afloat on the South China Sea in October 1982 who hailed their rescuers on the aircraft carrier *Midway*, "Hello, America sailor! Hello, freedom man!" As we prepare to celebrate the centennial of the Statue of Liberty, let all of us who love her cry out loud and clear, "Hello, freedom lady! Where liberty dwells, there is my country!"

God bless you.

Ronald Reagan

PREFACE
by Lee A. Iacocca

Whose parents were two of the many
welcomed to America by the Statue of Liberty

The Statue of Liberty has been a beacon for countless millions, and it still is recognized throughout the world as a symbol of hope and freedom. Ellis Island was the gateway to that freedom, a gateway through which sixteen million people during sixty-two years passed on their way to a new life. Almost half of all Americans alive today trace their roots to those who first set foot in America on Ellis Island.

This symbol of hope and this gateway to freedom are now being restored and all Americans should take part. By helping rebuild the Statue of Liberty and Ellis Island, we can show the world that our nation still values our ideals of freedom, hope, and hard work. And by bringing new life to these great symbols of America's heritage, we will honor not only these ideals, but also the sixteen million immigrants who passed their courage, faith, energy, and vitality on to their children and to America.

Lee A. Iacocca, Chairman of the Statue of Liberty-Ellis Island Centennial Commission and Chairman of the Board of Chrysler Corporation

Facing page: An immigrant family looking at the statue from Ellis Island in the early 1900s.

Our fathers' God! to Thee,
Author of liberty.
To Thee we sing:
Long may our land be bright
With freedom's holy Light;
Protect us by Thy might,
Great God, our King!
from "America"
Samuel F. Smith and Henry Carey

13

INTRODUCTION

As our troopship, the *General Harry Taylor*, steamed slowly through the Narrows of New York harbor that hot August afternoon in 1945, some three thousand of us, returning soldiers, jammed the rail eagerly watching for the one sight that would spell "home." All that day we had scanned the horizon, first catching sight of the distant New Jersey beaches shining in the sun. Then, as our ship moved into the broad shining harbor, it was easy to spot Manhattan's clustered spires looming in the far haze.

But our search was for something far more meaningful, something many of us had never seen before. For when we left this same harbor an eternity ago, it was in the middle of the night and there was a war-time blackout.

The excited chatter of the men ebbed. Then someone shouted: "There she is!" We craned our necks and squinted...and there she was. A stately woman in soft-green robes on the horizon lifting her lamp in welcome. It seemed as if a single sigh rose from three thousand emotion-tight throats.

We were home. We were finally home.

As the statue moved before us with the passage of our ship, I was surprised by her size. For most of my years I had carried a mental picture of her like the frontispiece of my grade-school history book. The scene portrayed an ocean liner's deck crowded with shawled immigrants gazing up in awe at a gigantic Statue of Liberty towering over them.

But the statue I now saw before me seemed so small in comparison. For a moment I wondered if the original had been temporarily replaced with a smaller model because of war hazards. But I dismissed the thought as ridiculous as I continued to study the graceful green lady now slipping into the mist as our ship entered the Hudson River.

Later, I learned that her creator had intended that she appear just as she was to arriving travelers. "I do not want her to dominate the harbor," he said. And so, like the gracious hostess she is, she greets her guests and family without overpowering them.

Everyone, it seems, has his own concept of our Statue of Liberty. It has been so since the beginning, as it was with each of the many unusual people who brought her to us. She was

- conceived in the heart of Édouard Laboulaye, French statesman, a Roman Catholic, who looked to America for his own country's salvation but never set foot on our shores.
- created by a French sculptor, Frédéric Auguste Bartholdi, a Protestant, who did not understand liberty until he saw it lost in his own land.

- strengthened through the ingenuity of Gustave Eiffel, French engineer, who became famous for another structure built later in his career.
- given a place to stand by Joseph Pulitzer, a Hungarian immigrant and would-be soldier, scorned and rejected by every major army in Europe.
- touched with a "soul of fire" by Emma Lazarus, a Jewish poet, who had turned her back on God until she saw Him at work among His people.

All of these people whose faiths and backgrounds represent a cross-section of America, I believe, were in one way or another inspired by the spiritual light that now symbolically burns in the torch our Statue of Liberty raises heavenward today.

Forty years after I first saw that torch welcoming me home, I returned to the statue as I have often done for a visit. It was a cold, gray day and even though the statue was cloaked under scaffolding for her renewal, hundreds of visitors waited to board the ferry that would take them to her.

Among the people who seemed to be in eager anticipation of their visit, I heard Kansas twangs, southern drawls, broad Yankee accents. I saw high-school jackets bearing names of cities in California, Florida, and Illinois. Japanese families took pictures of each other with the statue in the background. A turbaned Sikh escorted his sari-clad wife onto the boat as the public-address system welcomed the crowd in a variety of languages including French, German, Spanish, and Japanese.

What is it about her, I wondered, that excites the imagination? What is it that draws people from all over the world to Liberty Island?

In exploring our statue's colorful history I hope this book will answer these questions by telling the inspiring stories of the people who brought her to us.

Dick Schneider

From the very beginning, light seemed to symbolize our lady in the harbor.

One could say her spirit first caught fire when darkness rolled over the deep and God said, "Let there be light."

It was divine lightning that burned His Commandments for living on to the stone tablets Moses brought us from Mount Sinai.

It was His holy light that Christians believe blazed in the tomb that Easter morning, freeing mankind forever from the bonds of sin.

It is the light of truth and freedom by which man, whom He created in His own image and gave free will, was intended to live.

Historians speak of it burning in the eyes of a young French colonel, the Marquis de Lafayette, as he presented his heart and his sword to our Commander-in-Chief in 1777.

And men will always remember the blaze that swept the world after that April 14th night in 1865 when a derringer fired in the shadows of the presidential theater box.

All of these lights are fused into the flame that burns in the torch of our lady of liberty.

We also know that since the beginning, another force has been striving to extinguish that light, the only light by which man can truly live and achieve the potential God planned for him. Down through the ages we see it burning. We see it in the fire by night and the cloud by day as it led the Israelites through the wilderness to the Promised Land where they could worship God, unfettered and unoppressed.

It glows in the smoky cabin of the *Mayflower* gently rocking in the swells of a New World harbor as men labor over a compact pledging to support each other "in the name of God."

It flashes in the muskets of farmers and tradesmen at Concord and Lexington who battled for this new experiment in freedom. And when it was needed most, it was the light in the eyes of General Jean Baptiste Rochambeau who hurried from France to General George Washington's side. Without him, Lafayette, and his country's fleet of ships that helped ensure victory at Yorktown, the little torch of freedom might have flickered and died.

As the World Watched and Wondered

As it was, the world watched many lights begin to spread across the face of the new nation as it waxed and flourished. Until this age, no country had ever offered people this unique kind of democracy in which the rank and file governed themselves. And, as

THE LIGHT SEEN 'ROUND THE WORLD

the world continued to watch this new experiment in freedom of expression and worship, it wondered. Would it work?

However, a shadow fell on the western shore of the Atlantic. Slavery. It did not bother the wealthy and powerful in Europe as much as it did the working people who puzzled over it. If it weren't for this one blemish...

Then the light blazed again in the muzzles at Antietam and Gettysburg. And it burned deep in the eyes of a gawky giant who, more often than not, was scorned by the intelligentsia as "that gorilla" and "maniac." Not until the assassin's gun flashed in the Ford Theater and Abraham Lincoln was hurried to a house across the street to die, did the world realize how much he really meant to mankind everywhere. The loss of the man who said, "God must have loved the common man; He made so many of them," had a profound effect throughout the world, particularly on the common man who felt so close to him.

An Awesome Outpouring

"This sad event has moved the masses most intensely," observed a news correspondent in Europe. "They feel they have lost a friend, and humanity a benefactor."

In France the newly appointed American minister, John Bigelow, stood looking in awe at the mound of messages flooding his office desk. One was from a group of French youths who wrote that "three thousand of them would have wished to unite in a formal expression of their feelings if the police had not stopped them."

An hour earlier, a Gallic youth had brought a message from his own group:

> In President Lincoln we mourn a fellow citizen—for no country is now inaccessible, and we consider as ours that country where there are neither masters nor slaves, where every man is free or fighting to become free. We are the fellow citizens of John Brown, of Abraham Lincoln, and of Mr. Seward. We young people to whom the future belongs must have the courage to found a true democracy, and we shall have to look beyond the ocean to learn how a people who have made themselves free can preserve their freedom.

"I Had No Idea"

John Bigelow, who, himself, had often been concerned over Lincoln's lack of sovereignty, confessed in a letter to an associate back in America: "Familiar as I supposed I was with the currents of public opinion here towards the United States, I had no idea...."

As one report said:

> The people of France seemed to mourn...a figure embodying all that they long for and sometimes dare to believe in, such as a higher humanity than they had known and a freedom greater than their oppressions. They were stricken and sick at heart, shaken as they had not been in years. It was as though a light had gone out of the world for them, as though France, too, had been orphaned when Abraham Lincoln died....America had lost a president, but these people seemed to have lost a symbol of freedom.

Prophetic Three Words

Some weeks after the assassination, a small rural French newspaper, *Le Phare de la Loire*, suggested that a collection be taken for a gold medal to be presented to President Lincoln's widow.

To show that the medal was from the common people, donations were limited to not more than two cents. Even so, within just a few months, one of the paper's journalists proudly brought the finished medal to John Bigelow in his office. "Tell Mrs. Lincoln that in this little box is the heart of France," he said.

The United States minister picked up the gleaming medal and read its inscription: "Dedicated by French democracy to Lincoln, twice-elected President of the United States—honest Lincoln who abolished slavery, reestablished the Union, and saved the Republic, without veiling the statue of liberty."

Deeply moved, Bigelow thanked the young French journalist on behalf of his country, completely unaware, of course, as everyone else was at the time, of the implication of the inscription's last three words, a prophecy that would become reality twenty-one years in the future.

It took another Frenchman, Édouard René de Laboulaye, a gentle, eloquent, and deeply religious statesman, to set into motion a strange chain of events that would make those three prophetic words a living reality.

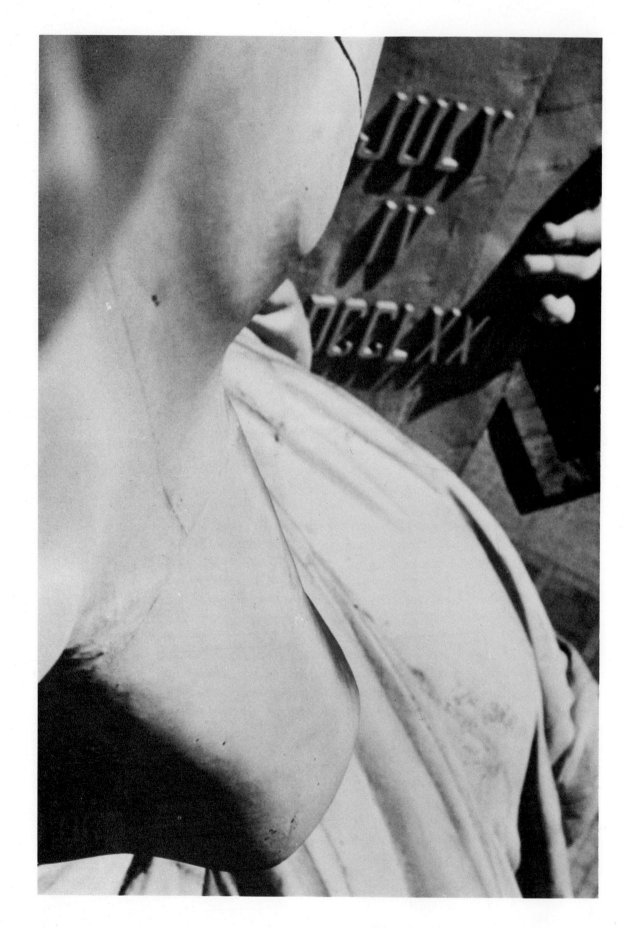

20

The Lombardy poplars were deepening to a dark mauve against a twilight sky that summer evening in 1865 in the little French village of Glatigny, when the first seed was sown. In a nearby chateau, windows glowed yellow from candlelight as a group of distinguished French statesmen, mellow from a sumptuous dinner, leaned back in their carved-wood chairs and discussed the state of affairs of their mother country.

All were well-known men such as the Count de Gasparin, the Christian moralist; M. Henri Martin, historian; and Charles de Remusat, the scholarly count. But none was more distinguished than the host, Édouard René Lefebvre de Laboulaye. And it was on him they focused their attention as in his gentle, melodious voice, he talked about a deepening mutual concern, the delicate relationship then existing between France and America, the country mourning its dead leader.

THE GOD-FATHER

The Man Who Loved America

Then in his fifties, the delicate olive-skinned gentleman with smooth brown hair was a distinguished professor of law, successful businessman, author, chairman of the French Anti-Slavery Society, and his country's most ardent champion of the United States.

Deeply religious, he was a devout Catholic who credited the start of his interest in America to reading a book by a Protestant theologian and abolitionist, Dr. William Ellery Channing of Boston.

Édouard de Laboulaye's apartment in Paris and country home in Glatigny were always open to American visitors, who immediately found themselves at home among their host's family, all of whom spoke English.

On the walls hung pictures of Washington, Jefferson, Franklin, Horace Mann, along with framed membership certificates in the New York and Philadelphia Union League clubs. Letters from Senator Sumner, Edward Everett, and James Russell Lowell lay on his desk, along with a note on Executive Mansion stationery signed "A. Lincoln."

His interest in America brought him many invitations to visit, but he would not step on a boat, even by the offer of eight thousand gold francs for a lecture tour. In referring to it, he said wistfully, "The French have never rated me that high."

An admirer of the American Revolution, he was always happy to talk about Lafayette whom he deeply respected. Some said that

Facing page: The statue's tablet, which reads "July 4, 1776."

Edouard René Lefebvre de Laboulaye, godfather to the Statue of Liberty.

Lafayette's mantle fell on Laboulaye's shoulders when, at the age of nineteen, he watched the old soldier on his white charger gallop through the streets of Paris in the July Revolution of 1830.

None of the revolutions, beginning with the French Revolution of 1789, had so far succeeded in bringing about the type of government that Laboulaye and his like-minded colleagues dreamed of. The more he studied the United States' Constitution, the more he hoped to help bring about a democratic government in his own country along the lines of that in America.

Daughter of the Gospel

Such a government offered real liberty, he felt. In his book *The Political History of the United States*, Laboulaye described true liberty as "the daughter of the Gospel—sister of justice and pity—mother of equality, abundance and peace."

He shrank from the French Revolution's cry of "The Age of Reason," reflected by the celebrated ride through Paris of a nude woman crowned as the "Goddess of Reason." The Revolution, he feared, had been taken over by atheists, was anti-Christian, and tended to mob rule.

He felt very differently about the War Between the States in America and watched it with deep concern. "Something told me," he wrote, "that God would not forsake a people fighting to free four million human beings, a people that stand for liberty in our world as Greece stood for art, and Rome for conquest and dominion."

Still, Laboulaye and his friends, many of whom were having dinner with him that night in Glatigny, were deeply loyal to France. Casting glances over their shoulders in the direction of the nearby palace at Versailles where the present dictator of France, Napoleon III, often visited, they worried about their country's bungling in the Western Hemisphere. Napoleon III, dissolute nephew of the famous general, was a despot and petty tyrant. In backing Austrian Archduke Maximilian's attempt to become emperor of Mexico, he had incurred the ire of the United States, helpless to intervene at the time because of the Civil War.

The men in Laboulaye's conservatory shook their heads as they talked of Napoleon III's stupidity. If Lincoln were still alive, they mourned, he would have curbed those in American government who hated France. He would have smoothed over the ruffled relations.

Gratitude Among Nations?

As brandy was sniffed and tobacco smoke rose from cigars and pipes, talk reportedly turned to the subject of gratitude between nations.

"There is no such thing," said one. He pointed to France's role in helping to save Italy's independence and protecting Rome from Garibaldi's revolutionaries. "And still that whole country seems to hate France."

"*Oui*," agreed a portly man as he flicked the ash from his cigar into a Limoges tray, "there is no such thing as gratitude among nations."

"Ah, but what about the United States?" another asked. "Certainly they remember Lafayette and Rochambeau?"

The portly man lifted his shoulders in a Gallic shrug. "The same," he sighed. "France cannot count on what we have done in the past."

There was a rustle at the head of the table as Édouard de Laboulaye rose to his feet. His eyes flashed and his voice lost its gentleness. "The United States has more sympathy for France than for any other European nation!" he is said to have declared.

The guests turned and looked to him with interest. Here was another speech from the popular college professor.

Laboulaye continued by pointing out that with Italy there had been no popular tradition of friendship. Yes, France aided the Italians in 1859, but in the end it was responsible for galling the Italians' memory.

France's help in the American Revolution was quite different, he maintained. America's feeling for France was founded on a common struggle in which Frenchmen who fought on the side of the colonists died for a principle they dreamed of seeing come alive in their own country.

A Fraternity of Feelings

"In that fight for independence," he said, "there was not simply a service to a friendly nation but a fraternity of feelings, a community of efforts and emotions; and when hearts have beaten together, something always remains—among nations as among individuals."

It was easy to see that a sensitive chord in Laboulaye had been touched; his guests listened attentively, their brandy snifters forgotten. When the professor was in this mood, new ideas were usually sparked.

Laboulaye said he was certain that Americans in general revered Lafayette and his volunteers for their heroic deeds in helping the colonists win their struggle for independence. He was certain that Americans remembered these heroes far more than any misguided political machinations of Napoleon III.

"There," he declared, "you have the basis of American feeling for the French—an indestructible basis!" He looked around at his guests and rapped the table for emphasis. "This feeling honors the Americans as well as us," he continued, "and if a monument should rise in the United States, as a memorial to their independence, I should think it only natural if it were built by a united effort—a common work of both of our nations."

Listening attentively at Laboulaye's table that night was a handsome young bearded man from Alsace-Lorraine. He was present because he had been commissioned to do some work for his host. And it was only natural that those last words of his host's speech should excite his interest in a special way, for he was an artist, a sculptor. His name was Frédéric Auguste Bartholdi.

Frédéric Auguste Bartholdi, the designer of the Statue of Liberty.

Frédéric Auguste Bartholdi leaned forward in his dining chair as Laboulaye's emotion-charged words rang out in the candle-lit room. An excitement churned within him for, of all the guests, this young bearded man with dark flashing eyes was most attuned to his host's challenge.

The handsome Alsatian was a sculptor who, at age thirty-one, had already distinguished himself. The word "monument" stirred him in particular for it signified immensity. And immensity was the hallmark of Bartholdi's unique calling.

Already his creations of war heroes and biblical figures towered against French horizons from his home city Colmar in the French province of Alsace to the Pyrenees Mountains. Grand themes in art had been his inspiration since his youth.

Bartholdi's father, a prosperous civil servant, had died when Frédéric was very young. His mother, Charlotte Beysser Bartholdi, a deeply religious woman and strong Protestant, had had a profound influence on the young artist, taking him to Paris where he studied under master artists. In later years she had moved back to Colmar where her son often visited her in the old family home on the rue des Marchands.

Though the young sculptor knew that an ancestor, the famous General Beysser of Ribeauville, was a hero of the French Revolution, his heart was set on artistic expression and the challenge of new horizons.

His passion for immensity in monuments was further fueled by a trip to Egypt where he looked up in awe at the gigantic Sphinx and excitedly focused his camera on the brooding seated figures of the Colossi at Thebes.

CRUCIBLE OF HER CREATOR

The Strength of the Idea

Bartholdi listened closely to a traveling companion, French painter Jean Gérôme, who said: "It is the strength of the idea which makes a work of art beautiful and lifts it beyond the demands of verisimilitude."

It was the strength of the idea in art, not politics, that fired Bartholdi's passion. Despite the rosette in his lapel identifying him as a Knight of the Legion of Honor earned by his patriotic creations, he was not overly concerned with governmental philosophies and man's fight for self-determination. Thus it was on that summer's night in 1865 in the Laboulaye dining room in Glatigny, though intrigued by the statesman's cry for a monument, he could not readily imagine what it should look like.

During the following months and years he found himself turning the idea over and over in his mind. What would symbolize the new American republic? Of the classic forms, he knew of none that represented independence.

In the meantime both Laboulaye and Bartholdi busily pursued their separate callings. The statesman concentrated on his teaching at the College de France and endeavored to help France become a real republic like the young nation he admired across the Atlantic. The sculptor continued fashioning new monuments and visited his mother often in his beloved Alsace. He discussed with her the dream he and Laboulaye shared. When Laboulaye campaigned in Alsace for a government post, Charlotte Beysser Bartholdi invited the graying professor to Colmar.

"The Lion of Belfort," by Bartholdi (built 1875-80). Besides the Statue of Liberty, perhaps his most famous work. It was a patriotic memorial to the town's heroic defenders against the Prussians in the Franco-Prussian War of 1870-71.

The Catholic and the Protestant

If he was expecting to meet a mousey, small-town widow, he would have been shocked by the tall, stately, silver-haired woman who glided down the steps to greet him. He could see why his young sculptor friend was so devoted to this lady with the royal carriage and classic features of a Roman noblewoman.

The Catholic statesman and the Protestant mother struck it off immediately, talking about the glory of the revolutionary wars for freedom, about the future of her beloved Alsace, and the rampant materialism which seemed to be taking over their country.

Meanwhile, Mme. Beysser Bartholdi's son was hotly pursuing another monumental challenge. On his Egyptian trip he had met countryman Ferdinand de Lesseps who would build the famous Suez Canal from the Mediterranean to the Red Sea. Struck by the magnitude of the project, he thought of the Colossus of Rhodes which he felt was the "most celebrated statue of antiquity." One of the seven legendary wonders of the ancient world, this huge bronze statue of the sun god, standing over a hundred feet high, had straddled the Rhodes harbor entrance.

What would be more suitable for the new canal, he thought, than to create a huge statue to serve as a lighthouse at its entrance? He envisioned towering over the canal a figure of an Egyptian peasant, a fellah, to portray the poor, anonymous laborers who had been toiling in Egypt for centuries. However, he had difficulty raising money for the project, and though he had prepared clay models, he had abandoned it by the time the canal was opened in 1869.

The Challenge of Glatigny

In the meantime Laboulaye's challenge of that summer evening in Clatigny continued to intrigue him, but the idea still defied artistic interpretation. He wondered if it was because he knew so little of America and the battle she had fought for liberty.
Most of the little he knew about the new republic stemmed from his friendship with an American, John La Farge. A law student in New York City, La Farge, about Bartholdi's age, had come to France to visit relatives. The two met in Paris, struck up a friendship, and kept in correspondence.

Invasion

In August 1870 Bartholdi's letter to La Farge in America was solemn. Spike-helmeted German troops had surged across the border into his homeland of Alsace which had long been a bone of contention between Germany and France. Suddenly, he found himself facing the cruel reality of war. Casting mallet and chisel aside, he threw himself into helping organize the Garde National militia. With a major's commission, he marched into battle with childhood friends carrying old rifles left over from the Revolution. Overpowered by a strong and highly organized enemy, he suffered blood and horror through a terrible winter. As he and his comrades wearily stumbled through town squares in retreat, he would often look up over his shoulder to see his own monuments etched against a smoky sky.

Finally, the French Provisional Government sued for an armistice and Alsace-Lorraine was ceded to Germany.

When Bartholdi morosely watched enemy troops march through his mother's home city of Colmar, he understood all too well why men give their lives for liberty.

He returned a different man to his Paris studio at 40, rue Vavin. Outside the quietness of his studio all of France was in confusion. The autocratic Napoleon III had fled into exile in England. Paris was slowly recovering from a mass revolt which had to be crushed by government troops. And men of varying beliefs competed for power while weary common folk longed for peace and stability.

When his old friend, Laboulaye, invited Bartholdi, along with several statesmen, to Glatigny in the spring of 1871, an atmosphere quite different from that gentle summer evening of six years earlier pervaded his host's dining room. Now, as cold spring raindrops ran in rivulets down the mullioned windows, the moderate Republicans sitting about the table gloomily wondered how they could achieve the longed-for "Third Republic." A new, more democratic government, it would be hopefully patterned after the United States.

As word of that young country across the Atlantic came up, Laboulaye raised his glass to it, saying "that without any doubt there would be at the hundredth anniversary of the Independence of the United States, a movement patriotic and French in America!"

Looking about the table, he asked: Would this not be an appropriate time for the monument he had proposed six years ago?

Chairs scraped back as the men turned to each other in excitement. But of course! Brandy and cigars were forgotten as the men discussed Laboulaye's suggestion. Would not a magnificent monument to liberty weld a bond between France and the United States, which had just emerged from its own war to make men free?

A Unifying Symbol!

Heads nodded enthusiastically. Not only that, but it would stand out as a unique symbol, unifying their own countrymen when it was most needed. And suddenly the import of it all seemed to strike everyone at once. What could be better in advancing the cause of the Third Republic, the new France!

As the excited conversation waxed about the project, one man was silent. Perhaps his mind was remembering the dinner six years ago and the talk of the gold medal struck for Abraham Lincoln's widow, the medal inscribed "Dedicated by French democracy...without veiling the statue of liberty."

Finally Bartholdi spoke. Leaning back in his chair, he said he had already thought of the kind of monument that should be offered.

The room fell quiet as his companions leaned forward attentively.

"I think it would be well to offer the Americans a statue," he is reported to have said. "A statue of Liberty."

There were warm murmurs of approval.

Yes, marvelous. But what kind of statue had he in mind?

"If possible," he said, his dark eyes twinkling, "it ought to be a statue that can be seen from the shores of America to the coast of France."

The room exploded in laughter and hand clapping.

"Go See That Country!"

Laboulaye and Bartholdi looked at each other. Both knew what the other was thinking. Laboulaye had seen small clay models on which Bartholdi had been working in his studio on rue Vavin. And they had already discussed it.

Now Laboulaye put the next step into a ringing declamation. "Go see that country," he urged the sculptor. "You will study it, you will bring back to us your impressions. Propose to our friends over there to make with us a monument, a common work, in remembrance of the ancient friendship of France and the United States!"

Applause broke out around the table.

"We will take up a subscription in France," continued Laboulaye. He looked at the men around the table who nodded in assent. Turning back to Bartholdi he added, "If you find a happy idea, a plan that will excite public enthusiasm, we are convinced that it will be successful on both continents, and we will do a work that will have a far-reaching moral effect!"

Again Laboulaye's oratory inspired an audience. And on that day in Glatigny there flamed the renewed spirit of a great republic as the room rang with exclamations of approval for the statue of "liberty enlightening the world!"

A New Bartholdi

The man to whom Laboulaye directed his challenge was far different from the young dilettante who had sat at his table that summer's evening six years ago. Lines etched his face, furrows put there by grim fighting in snowbound passes, sorrow from watching his boyhood friends die beside him. This was a man who knew what victory cost. Even more, he knew what the absence of liberty cost as he thought about his mother existing, virtually a prisoner, in an enemy-occupied town now called Kolmar.

A month later, armed with letters of introduction, he traveled to Le Havre and boarded the SS *Pereire* on his first voyage to America. Before closing his studio on the rue Vavin, he sat down, took up a pen, and wrote a message to Laboulaye. "I will try to glorify the Republic and Liberty over there, in the hope that someday I will find it again here."

It was a rough crossing.

For almost two weeks the little steamship SS *Pereire* pitched and rolled through the gale-swept seas of the north Atlantic that cold June of 1871. Many passengers were violently ill but the *mal de mer* did not quench Frédéric Bartholdi's enthusiasm. As his cabin paneling groaned and spray lashed the porthole, the sculptor pored over guidebooks and maps of the immense country he was about to visit.

Even so, he had little concept of the new world, scant knowledge of its culture, not even an idea yet for the location of the statue which had inspired this journey. And no guidebook could prepare him for what he was about to experience.

It happened on the morning of June 21 when the *Pereire* finally steamed into the smooth waters of the Narrows, the long inlet into New York City's spacious harbor.

BIRTH PAINS AND TRAVAILS

A Special Morning

On awakening to the unusual calmness, Bartholdi rubbed his eyes and peered out the porthole to see rolling green hills sweeping down to the Narrows' shores. The peaceful countryside was dotted with houses, farms, and patches of woods. As his ship slowed to pick up its harbor pilot, Bartholdi quickly threw on his clothes, heart pounding.

He raced up a companionway to the mist-damp deck and rushed to the rail to better see the country he had heard so much about. Now almost forty years old he felt as excited as a child on Christmas morning as he eagerly peered through the morning mist.

Then, as the sun climbed higher, the mist lifted to reveal the vast panorama of the sparkling harbor. The sculptor gasped and gripped the rail, for as he later wrote:

> The picture that is presented to the view when one arrives at New York is marvelous. When—after some days of voyaging—in the pearly radiance of a beautiful morning is revealed the magnificent spectacle of those immense cities....

Impressed by New York City and Brooklyn, soon to be connected by the Brooklyn Bridge then under construction, his eye caught the silver sweep of the Hudson and East rivers. The hooting and bellowing of ships, tugs, and small boats crisscrossing the harbor filled his ears.

As he stood at the rail drinking in his first view of the New

World, memories from the past must have swept before him, of a stricken Paris under siege, of men dying alongside him for liberty, of his mother living under the dominion of enemy troops. But here before him was the very picture of freedom. *Here*, in this harbor, he decided, his heart lifting, was the perfect site for his statue!

"May God Be Pleased"

"The Statue was born for this place which inspired its conception," he later wrote, almost in prayer. "May God be pleased to bless my efforts and my work and to crown it with the success, the duration and moral influence which it ought to have."

It was decided.

"Yes," he enthused, "in this very place shall be raised the statue of Liberty, as grand as the idea which it embodies, casting radiance upon the two worlds."

It was with this vision that Bartholdi, also a painter, quickly sketched a view of how he felt his statue should appear in the harbor. In it a classically-robed woman with radiant crown soars against the sky from a small island. Her right hand raises a torch to heaven while her left bears a tablet such as the one Moses carried down from Mount Sinai.

With the chuffing of tugs and shouts of dock workers, the *Pereire* was eased to its Hudson River pier.

Could the Dream Become Reality?

"I have found the idea which my friends had hoped for," wrote the voyager. He then stepped down the gangplank onto American soil to "see whether the dream could become reality."

After passing through customs, he hailed a horse-drawn cab and was immediately swallowed up in the bustle of New York streets, already suffering grid lock in 1871. Giant Percherons heaved at drays groaning under bricks for new buildings which seemed to be rising everywhere. Delivery wagons clattered over cobblestones. And the sidewalks were alive with people hurrying on what seemed to be important errands.

He remembered Laboulaye's capsulization of the New World: "Freedom to do anything, dare anything, try anything—there you have the American social principle!"

Yes, thought Bartholdi as his driver fought through an intersection, his old friend's description was very apt.

In his hotel the traveler opened his trunk and sorted through his many letters of introduction to American dignitaries given to him by his friends and sponsors.

One name, however, for which he needed no introduction was his old friend John La Farge whom he had met sixteen years earlier in Paris. The two had kept up correspondence and Bartholdi knew that La Farge was now a family man who had since left law practice to devote himself to painting. They had a joyful reunion. But when Bartholdi began calling on those to whom he had been given introductions, he did not find the same warm reception for his Statue of Liberty. Horace Greeley, editor of the New York *Tribune*, and Cyrus Field, who had laid the Atlantic cable, listened to his proposal but offered no real help, probably because it seemed to offer little material gain.

A Small Island Off of Manhattan

However, Bartholdi did decide on what he felt was the best location for the Statue of Liberty. He had originally chosen Governor's Island near the city but discarded that site as it would mean that the statue would turn her back on New York. Instead, he picked a small island about a mile and a half southeast of the tip of Manhattan.

Called Bedloe's Island after its original owner, Isaack Bedlow, who had emigrated to New Amsterdam from Calais, France, before 1664, it later bore the names Love Island (after governor Lovelace), Oyster, and Kennedy's.

As he wrote: "Today, after a little sketching for projects, I went to the harbor to visit the island which will serve as a base for the monument, and which is in a situation admirably suited to what I want to execute."

In what way "admirably suited"? Undoubtedly, he chartered a small boat and made several trips along the route taken by incoming ocean vessels into this "main gateway to the New World." And he envisioned the statue's effect on the immigrant who would see it on Bedloe's Island as the ship made the long curving run from the harbor entrance at the Narrows to lower Manhattan. In this way, he believed, the statue would be admired best.

He also liked this location since, being situated in a harbor twenty square miles in area, the statue would not overpower the viewer but would appear "simply in harmony with the whole, and have the normal aspect of a statue in a public square."

On the island rose what could be a natural foundation for the statue's pedestal, the star-shaped ramparts of Fort Wood (named for Colonel Eleazar Wood, a hero of the War of 1812). The fort had been built in 1811 on even earlier bulwarks to protect the main channel of New York Harbor.

More excited than ever about the project, he added: "I believe that this undertaking will take very great proportion and, if things turn out the way I think, this work of sculpture will take on a very great moral significance."

Right then Bartholdi dubbed this site "Liberty Island," not knowing, of course, that this would become its official name generations later.

On the President's Front Porch

Besides selecting the statue's location and getting to know New York, the sculptor made the most of his east coast contacts. He used one of his letters of introduction to visit President Ulysses S. Grant in his summer White House in Long Branch, New Jersey. For a half-hour the two sat on the homey front porch of the two-story frame house overlooking the blue Atlantic. The president, smoking a long black cigar, listened to Bartholdi tell about his dream, nodded thoughtfully, but offered no direct encouragement.

Undaunted, the sculptor traveled on to Philadelphia to meet Colonel John W. Forney, publisher of the Philadelphia *Press*; then on to hot, humid Washington, D.C. where he was welcomed enthusiastically by Massachusetts Senator Charles Sumner, a long time friend of Laboulaye's and a fiery abolitionist.

But Congress was out of session in summer and after a short time Bartholdi traveled north to Boston. Here he felt very much at home among the quaint buildings and academic atmosphere. Again he found himself sitting on a front porch looking out to sea, in company of a famous personage. Henry Longfellow had invited him to lunch at his summer home in Nahant, Massachusetts. Unlike Grant, the poet was enthusiastic about the project and the sculptor noted that when they parted, Longfellow "pressed my hand as if he wished electrically to convey that pressure to his friends in France, charging me to express to them all his enthusiasm for their plans."

A Poet Charmed

Longfellow appears charmed too. As he inscribed in his journal:

M. Auguste Bartholdi, French sculptor, calls...a pleasant, lively, intelligent man, a Republican and an Alsatian. He has a plan for erecting a bronze Colossus on Bedloe's Island, in New York Harbor—a statue of liberty, to serve at night as a lighthouse. It is a grand plan; I hope it will strike the New Yorkers.

But the New Yorkers showed little interest except for those in the French community. It was time, Bartholdi felt, that he obey Laboulaye's charge and "go see the country." Taking a carriage to Commodore Vanderbilt's new Grand Central Depot at Twenty-sixth Street, he boarded the first train west.

On the Road

On August 12 he stopped at Niagara Falls where, like every other tourist, he had a photo taken of himself with the falls in the background. And then he found himself in "the most American city" he had ever seen. To think, he wrote home in 1871, that in 1804 Chicago had only five residents while today there are almost 300,000 plus 126 churches and about 100 newspapers. As he watched Chicagoans dashing about, urged on by the "stomach-ache of business," he concluded that it was a marvelous place to visit but he would certainly not want to live there. In another few months much of the city he saw was destroyed in the great Chicago fire.

But this still was not the America he wanted to see. His wishes began to be satisfied when his rattling railroad coach pulled out of Omaha, Nebraska.

"At a short distance from Omaha starts the Prairie," he noted. "...It becomes wilder and wilder as one approaches the Rocky Mountains until it finally looks like a desert....In spite of this, one can find a certain charm in this immensity which is like the sea."

As he stood on the observation car's platform, wind ruffling his long dark hair and cinders smudging his Parisian suit, he stared at the immensity which was broken only occasionally by a railroad station and small clusters of houses.

A fellow passenger pointed out the remnants of the wagon trail of the pioneers who had headed west and he was particularly touched. "This old trail is only indicated by a few dusty ruts," he wrote. "It is like a large path—it is the track painfully made on the soil by countless migrants who dragged themselves for months in those vast expanses."

"Sights of Savageness"

More and more he was sensing the deeper meaning of the country that lured settlers from all over the world. And he could hardly believe that so many of them had crossed the Rocky Mountains.

"At the entrance to these mountains there are sights of extraordinary savageness...red masses of rock extravagantly shaped, burnt terrains, grey grass, red moss, no trees, dried up torrents....There are some diabolical sights as in fairy tales."

Fascinated, he could not wait to see more. At a stop in Salt Lake City he met the famed Mormon leader, Brigham Young, who asked him to paint his portrait. But Bartholdi was in a hurry to press on. And soon his train descended into California where "one enters valleys and gorges, one passes through trenches and tunnels from one ravine to the other, skirting enormous masses of rocks. Some of the sights are magnificent."

And then he was standing on the shore of San Francisco Bay, looking into the blue haze of the Pacific. Here, as in the other cities he visited, he tried to organize committees and correspondents for the mammoth project but found little enthusiasm among those to whom New York harbor was of little concern.

Undaunted, he returned east, gaping at a gigantic herd of buffalo thundering in the distance on the Great Plains, fascinated by the wild wooded lands in the midwest where trees were already being touched golden by frost, marveling at magnificent bridges soaring from one mountainside to another.

Traveling Salesman

"As you see," he wrote his friend Laboulaye, "I have drawn out my journey beyond my original plan. I am making a veritable missionary's tour, not always amusing but very interesting. In every town I look for people who may wish to take part in our enterprise. So far, I have found them everywhere; the ground is well prepared." At this point he undoubtedly stopped writing for a moment, pressed the end of his pen to his bearded chin, and looking at cold, hard facts realized that "only the spark will have to be provided by a manifestation on the part of France."

Back east, he went right to Washington where he was received at the White House, shook hands with senators, and met many generals, including Sherman and Sheridan. And again, he found no concrete evidence of practical help for this project.

By the time Bartholdi was ready to return to France in late 1871, he knew that he had not achieved his original purpose. There was interest in the statue, yes. But there was no general outpouring of emotion on the part of Americans.

However, Bartholdi had achieved his most important goal, the one referred to by Laboulaye in his ringing speech in Glatigny: "Go see the country and bring us back your impressions."

A Measure of America

Now he had a measure of the country itself. He had traveled its mammoth stretch from sea to sea, had met its people from the bootblack on Broadway to the socialite on Nob Hill.

He had found that:

America was a melting pot, not just a mixture of nationalities, but of ideas, characteristics, philosophies, a crucible of new humanity. Nothing was cut and dried....The very freedom of the New World seemed a matter of space, of growth, of bigness. It knew no bounds because it knew no bounds. Without limits, it did not need limitations.[1]

Yes, Bartholdi had gained a vision from his journey, a vision that would truly shape his statue in ways that he could not foresee. But as his ship left New York harbor that final day and he stood at the rail watching his "Liberty Island" fade into the mist, he knew that he had nothing concrete to bring home to Laboulaye and the other men at Glatigny, no signed documents of approval, no popular subscription of funds.

And yet, he probably did not realize that from a practical standpoint he had made two very important contacts.

One was a charming young French girl, Jeanne-Emilie Baheux de Puysieux, a cousin of John La Farge. Orphaned at six, she had been adopted by a Canadian woman who happened to be visiting with the La Farges in Newport when Bartholdi came by.

The other person was Richard Hunt. Hunt was an architect who had worked on the Louvre Library Pavilion in Paris which Bartholdi knew well.

What was Hunt doing now? Bartholdi inquired.

Oh, building mansions for wealthy Americans, he reportedly answered, adding that artistic structures were more to his liking.

---

[1]Hertha Pauli and E. B. Ashton, *I Lift Up My Lamp* (New York: E. P. Dutton, 1948), 108.

It is said that the two discussed pedestals such as those supporting Bartholdi's many creations throughout Europe and their vital importance in complementing the work they supported.

Bartholdi undoubtedly had other thoughts on his mind as the shores of his new found friend, America, finally faded from sight. The most important of which being: Would his Statue of Liberty ever grace that great harbor?

When he returned to France he was met by conditions that made the possibility seem even more remote.

A Desolate Homeland

When Bartholdi's ship reached Le Havre that icy, wintry day in 1872, he disembarked onto a saddened homeland still in turmoil. Spike-helmeted, gray-clad troops would occupy eastern France for another year. Enemy soldiers were bad enough, but as his carriage rattled over cobblestones in Paris his heart sank in dismay at the sight of the charred ruins lining the boulevard. For Bartholdi knew it was caused by Frenchmen fighting Frenchmen. In 1871 the volatile Parisians, angered at the monarchists for accepting a humiliating peace with Prussia, set up their own communal government. A raging civil war ensued and the monarchists had retreated to Versailles.

Howling mobs of *Communards* burned the Tuileries Palace, the Louvre, the Palace of Justice, and shot hostages left and right. The Versaillais monarchists charged back into Paris executing thousands of men, women, and children.

Finally, seeing an uneasy peace and a provisional government in control, Bartholdi and Laboulaye sadly agreed that this was not the time to be talking about France giving a statue of "liberty enlightening the world." Not until France achieved a moderate republican form of government, they felt, could this be done.

In the meantime both men had other work to do.

The Monument Maker

Bartholdi busied himself with commissioned works, including a grand monumental fountain for the 1876 Philadelphia Centennial Exhibition; a tower frieze for a Boston church illustrating Christian baptism, communion, marriage, and death; a statue of Lafayette which France would present to New York for its war relief efforts; and one of his most famous works, the Lion of Belfort.

It, too, commemorated liberty, honoring the valiant people of Belfort, a city in Alsace, who had stubbornly withstood a Prussian siege. Moved by their heroism, Prussia allowed Belfort and its surrounding area to remain free. Bartholdi's huge wounded lion, a shattered spear under one paw, still today roars defiance from its stone mountainside.

Laboulaye, now quite elderly, was just as busy in turbulent French politics. The gentle republican professor found himself between two factions fighting to control France, the revolutionary *Communards* and the monarchist sympathizers. He had viewed the American Revolution as a just struggle by religious men, but his own country's revolution bothered him because he felt it was led by atheists. And though he feared the *Communards* as anti-Christians tending to mob rule, he also opposed the monarchists as insensitive to the populace and illiberal.

Uniting Two Frances

However, he knew that the two Frances must become one, under an orderly government representing the people—a republic. As had Abraham Lincoln, he remembered Jesus' admonition that "every city or house divided against itself will not stand" (Matt. 12:25).

To reunite France he threw himself into a campaign waged in the provisional National Assembly. In speech after impassioned speech he pleaded for a constitution around which every citizen could rally. Holding out his hands in supplication he cried, where was their sense of duty? their honor? their responsibility?

"Have pity," he begged, in one final speech, voice tremoring, "have pity on France!"

The Assembly was silent when he slumped into his chair, emotionally drained. Some deputies wiped their eyes, and, amid a rustling of silks and starched ruffles, many rose in tribute.

Two days later, January 30, 1875, an amendment which began "The President of the Republic..." was passed, 353 to 352. Laboulaye's republicans had won and the Third French Republic was in existence. Now, with the American Constitution in mind, he sat down to write the new French Constitution.

A Dream Takes Shape

Meanwhile, his dream of a statue of liberty for America had continued to burn in his heart. A year earlier, 1874, he and other enthusiasts had quietly formed the *Union Franco-Américaine* to bring their dream into reality. The committee included descendants of Lafayette, Rochambeau, and Alexis de Tocqueville, whose famous study, *Democracy in America*, predicted democracy's triumph. Laboulaye was elected president.

The committee did not remain quiet for long. On September 28, 1875, they published an appeal in French newspapers asking citizens to contribute to the statue. It read, in part:

> The great event which is to be celebrated on the 4th of July, 1876, allows us to celebrate with our American brothers the old and strong friendship which for a long time has united the two peoples.

> The New World is preparing to give extraordinary splendor to that festival. Friends of the United States have thought that the genius of France ought to display itself in a dazzling form. A French artist has embodied that thought in a plan worthy of its object, and which is approved by all; he has come to an understanding with our friends in America and has prepared all the means for executing the plan.

> It is proposed to erect, as a memorial of the glorious anniversary, an exceptional monument. In the midst of the harbor of New York, upon an islet which belongs to the Union of the States, in front of Long Island, where was poured out the first blood for independence, a colossal statue would rear its head....

> ...We will in this way declare by an imperishable memorial the friendship that the blood spilled by our fathers sealed of old between the two nations....

Their vision was a cooperative effort of two countries—the statue to be constructed and shipped across the Atlantic by the French people, and the pedestal supporting it to be designed and built by the American people.

When the Republic of France was on its way to becoming a reality, Laboulaye wrote an open letter to the United States which was published in the New York *Tribune*, October 15, 1875, in which he stated that his country wished to take part in America's Centennial of Independence and celebrate "that noble liberty which represents the glory of the United States, and which enlightens the modern people by its example."

Off and Running

The official launching of the fund-raising campaign was celebrated with a magnificent banquet on November 6, 1875, at the Grand Hotel du Louvre in Paris. Some two hundred guests dined on fourteen courses under a red, white, and blue ceiling of French and American flags. One end of the hall displayed a huge illuminated painting of the statue as it would appear at night in New York's harbor.

Both French and American reporters furiously filled notebooks as the great hall rang with glowing declarations of French-American friendship from the various speakers. One was Washburne, the American minister in Paris; also Colonel Forney from Philadelphia; and, of course, Édouard Laboulaye.

By the time the banquet ended, pledges had already been made toward the statue's estimated cost of $250,000. (It would end up costing $400,000 due to construction difficulties.)

A Country Responds

Gallic hearts throughout France were touched and donations poured in from over a hundred thousand citizens, plus 181 city and town governments. Special benefits were held, authorized models of the statue were sold, and the famous composer, Gounod, created a *Liberty* cantata which was presented at the Paris Grand Opera.

At the premiere of the cantata, Laboulaye, in a speech, pointed out the difference between this Liberty and the one portrayed in Delacroix's famed painting of the revolutionary barricades. "This Liberty will not be the one wearing a red bonnet on her head, a pike in her hand, who walks on corpses," he promised. "It will be the American Liberty who does not hold an incendiary torch, but a beacon which enlightens."

With funds pouring in, Bartholdi was now able to begin realizing his exciting vision conceived that sunny morning when he first sailed into New York harbor.

Never in history had a statue as large as this one been built. And its creation would be an adventure in itself, full of surprises and little miracles.

Just what went into the design of Miss Liberty which, next to the American flag, more than anything else personifies the United States in the eyes of the world?

Much information on her background stems from the sculptor's own words. The rest is educated conjecture based on what we know about Bartholdi and his interests.

Obviously he was influenced by early conceptions of what man has called "the spirit of liberty" dating back to antiquity. In ancient Rome liberty was portrayed as a robed woman grasping a scepter connoting self-rule, a crushed vase-of-confinement at her feet, and wearing the Phrygian cap that was given to slaves when awarded their freedom.

GENESIS OF MISS LIBERTY

The Light of Faith

As a student of sculpture, Bartholdi undoubtedly studied Cesare Ripa's Renaissance portrait of Faith (*Fede Cattolica*) in Perugia, Italy. It portrays a white-gowned classical woman lifting high a heart bearing a flaming candle symbolizing the light of faith in extinguishing the darkness of ignorance and superstition. In her left arm she carries both an open New Testament and tablets of the Old Testament.

Down through the centuries paintings and statues of figures representing liberty have been shown lifting lighted torches high.

But probably the work that signified liberty most in the eyes of the French people was Delacroix's famous painting done in 1830 to commemorate the French Revolution—*28 Juillet, La Liberté guidant le peuple aux barricades*. It shows a powerful classic female striding forward through battle, brandishing the French tricolor in her right hand and a rifle in the other. Her Hellenistic gown hangs loosely from her waist and she wears the classic Phrygian bonnet while, stepping over corpses of fallen fighters, she urges her followers onward. The shaky French government of the 1830s felt this painting to be so inflammatory that it was barred from public exhibition until 1874, when the moderate republicans then in sway felt it was safe enough to display in the Louvre.

Statues of Faith

But it seems evident that Bartholdi was strongly influenced by religious themes in statuary. For example, in his travels through northern Italy he might well have seen Santo Varni's marble statue of *Faith* in the Staglieno cemetery of Genoa which, towering some thirty feet high, portrays a classically-clad woman with a radiant crown, holding a cross in her right hand and a Bible in her left.

Bartholdi probably saw a number of similar statues representing faith and religion in Italy and many of these have a radiant crown, probably representing a spiritual halo.

The halo can be seen on the head of the ancient sun god Helios who, in Greek mythology, left his eastern palace every morning in a golden chariot drawn by four immortal horses for his second home in the west. In the city of Rhodes, he was the national god, and the storied Colossus of Rhodes, representing him, which straddled the harbor entrance, also had a radiant crown symbolizing the sun's radiance to the seven planets.

Radiance of Faith

This theme was picked up by sculptors through the centuries and adorned statues of Constantine, the first Christian Roman emperor, and a number of state monuments in France.

Interestingly, the Bartholdi family emblem was a radiant sunburst dating back to his paternal great-grandfather who took over his wife's family business, the "Maison Sonntag."

In the Statue of Liberty, we know that her seven radiant beams "enlighten" the seven continents and seven seas of the world.

As Bartholdi's early clay models emerged, we can see changes made, some of which reflected the above antecedents. For example, his first model showed a broken vase in her left hand, a reference to the ancient symbol of liberty, then a broken chain which was transferred to her feet, and finally the large tablet bearing the Roman numerals for July 4, 1776.

In the Mosaic Tradition

In referring to the tablet, Marvin Trachtenberg in his enlightening book *The Statue of Liberty* says:

Although shields and open books were common sculptural devices for displaying inscriptions, stone tablets were comparatively rare. When not in the hands of Moses himself they generally embody a Mosaic reference, as in figures of the Synagogue and Faith who usually display the Old Law on a tablet. Liberty's tablet—particularly the way it is borne forward—is an unmistakable allusion not only to political events but to the great Mosaic tradition. And, indeed, not only does she carry the tablet of the patriarch but her radiant crown also may allude to the "rays of light" about his face after the revelation. Thus she is, along with everything else, a seer

Bartholdi's mother, Charlotte, whose face was the model for the statue's face.

and a prophetess. Considered in this way, her tablet bears not so much a remembrance as an implicit commandment—Seek Liberty!—and a prophecy: Liberty, as achieved in America in 1776, shall spread throughout the world, and most importantly, to France.[1]

Reflecting the challenge to "Seek Liberty" is the statue's face, most distinct from the bland visages of many other works. For Miss Liberty's face is real, modeled after Bartholdi's own mother whom he so deeply loved and respected, and for whom he grieved as being virtually a prisoner in her Alsace homeland.

It seems fitting that the statue that stands at our nation's gate represents a combination of many symbols of liberty preceding her, just as the millions of immigrants she has welcomed have combined their varying national traits, talents, and gifts into the mainstream of America, making our country so richly blessed.

[1]Marvin Trachtenberg, *The Statue of Liberty* (New York: Viking Penguin, 1976), 79.

So far, the Statue of Liberty was only a clay model a little over four feet high in Bartholdi's studio. How would one enlarge it to a statue as tall as a fifteen-story building, one that would be strong enough to withstand the corrosive salt air and gales that swept across New York harbor?

As the sculptor pondered these questions, he knew that the traditional method of casting it from metal was out of the question. Such a heavy statue, even broken down in sections, would be almost impossible to ship, much less erect.

However, he remembered the ancient *repoussé* technique in which the legendary Colossus of Rhodes was said to have been built. In it thin sheets of malleable metal were thought to have been hammered into shape and then riveted together over a firm interior such as wood or stone. He remembered from one of his trips through Italy standing on the shores of Lago Maggiore and looking up at the towering statue of an Italian saint, Carlo Borromeo. It had been made with the *repoussé* method using thin copper sheets freely supported on iron beams. Copper, he knew, was resistant to corrosion and relatively soft and malleable. He would do the same for Liberty.

OVER THE ROOFTOPS OF PARIS

Work Begins

The only workshop with the facilities that he knew for producing such a project was Gaget, Gautheir et Cie in Paris. Craftsmen in their mammoth workshop at 25, rue de Chazelles had created the imposing statues surmounting the spires of Notre Dame cathedral. The contract was let and work begun.

With his four-foot model of Liberty as a guide, Bartholdi made a plaster one over nine feet tall. From it he then made an even larger one of plaster which towered thirty-six feet, the height of a three-story building. Supported by framework, it was one quarter of the size of the final statue. With each enlargement he carefully refined the dimensions and form of Liberty to make sure she retained her proper effect.

Now came the most difficult part: translating it all into the final statue. He began by dividing the surface of the thirty-six-foot-high form into some 300 separate areas such as an elbow, part of a cheek, or fold of gown. Each section was then enlarged four times in size by the precise mathematical process called "pointing up." This required some 9,000 separate calculations for each part. Measurements were made back and forth from points on the plaster model's surface to related points on an enlarged matching area

Facing page: The statue's head was on display in this Paris park while the rest of the statue was being finished.

molded into corresponding shape by using thin strips of yielding wood, finally smoothed and hardened under a coat of plaster.

In the end Bartholdi had 300 of these large shaped plaster sections which, theoretically, could be assembled into a full-size statue.

Strong laminated wooden molds were then made from these plaster sections. These 300 molds were used to shape the individual sheets of copper.

The hand and arm frame under construction in Bartholdi's Paris workshop. Bartholdi is in the lower right corner (without hat).

Workmen in the Paris shop with various models of the statue.

Robe Thick as a Silver Dollar

Each sheet was about the thickness of a silver dollar. Craftsmen would hoist one into the mold and force it into proper shape by pressing with levers and beating with hammers. For complicated surfaces such as the folds in Liberty's gown, the copper had to be heated until it was soft and malleable. When the formed sheet was lifted out of its wood mold, men then hammered its outer surface to bring out fine details such as hair and eyebrows.

The copper itself was a symbol of French homes. "It is known," reported the *Courier des Etats-Unis*, "that one generous subscriber, a great Parisian merchant, will give all the copper needed for the statue."

Though the news item stated that the contributor wished to remain anonymous, it was fairly obvious that the firm was a local

51

hardware establishment, Japy Fréres, whose copper cookware gleamed from the white-washed walls of almost every French kitchen.

The giant, formed parts, themselves shining with the brilliance of madame's polished pans, were feather-edged so they could be fitted together with one-fifth-inch flush-headed copper rivets.

Her "Awful Eye"

Some of the parts were joined together into units immediately so detailing could be better completed on the spot. In describing work on Liberty's head, a correspondent for the New York *World* wrote:

The statue's head on display at the Paris Exhibition of 1878. The exhibition building was designed by Eiffel. From a lithograph at the Musée Bartholdi, Colmar.

The workshop was built wholly and solely for the accommodation of this one inmate and her attendants, some 50 workmen hammering for their lives on sheer copper to complete the toilet of her tresses for the show. The Lilliputians reached her back hair by means of ladders running from stage to stage of a high scaffolding. I mounted the scaffolding with them and stood on a level with her awful eye—some 30 inches from corner to corner—to be ingulfed in her gaze.

The workmen were rushing to complete both Liberty's head and torch-bearing forearm with the purpose of these two elements being used not only as fund-raisers, but to maintain interest in the project which would be years in building.

The statue's hand and torch on display at the Philadelphia Exhibtion of 1876.

A Headful of Sightseers

Her head was sent to the Paris International Fair of 1878 where, displayed in front of the Exposition Building, she gazed serenely at the horizon. Fair-goers eagerly lined up to climb interior steps to the platform inside her crown where as many as forty people rubbing shoulders could look out the rectangular windows of her diadem.

And though Liberty's body was far from being ready for America's 1876 Centennial, she was there in spirit via her right hand and torch. It was sent to the United States where it was a highlight of the Philadelphia Centennial exposition. Again, climbing it was the attraction and visitors mounted a ladder inside the wrist to emerge from a trap door onto the balcony encircling the torch where as many as twelve people could stand.

So popular was it that, after the Philadelphia Centennial, it was shipped to New York City where it was erected on Madison Square, near Fifth Avenue and Twenty-third Street, then a prestigious hotel district (one hostelry was named "Bartholdi"). It became a popular tourist attraction and stood there for seven years until 1884, when it was sent back to France for installation on the soon-to-be-completed Liberty.

Meanwhile, amid the continual cloud of dust at rue de Chazelles in Paris, where Liberty was under construction, Bartholdi wrestled with a problem. How best to support his thin-skinned figure from within its interior? He knew that the huge Carlo Borromeo statue he saw in Italy was filled with a massive masonry core. He rejected that as too cumbersome.

"Fill Her with Sand"

His engineer, the eminent Eugéne Emmanuel Viollet-le-Duc, recommended that the statue's interior be compartmentalized and filled with sand, rising to at least her hips. However, he died in 1879 before anything could be done. The delay was fortuitous, for responsibility for its structural support passed into the hands of a genius, Gustave Eiffel, a man who had studied chemistry but whose spirit was led to engineering.

Already he had introduced new concepts in structural design, soaring airy railroad bridges stronger than any yet developed, and

Gustave Eiffel, the famous architect-engineer who designed the statue's interior support structure.

The scaffolding in place for the erection of the statue in Paris.

graceful skyscraping iron pylons that would later trademark his most famous creation, the Eiffel Tower built in 1889.

Interestingly, in view of Liberty's "mother figure," Eiffel shared a common blessing with Bartholdi in that he, too, had an energetic, courageous mother whom he deeply loved and admired. The two men found material inspiration in each other; and without Eiffel's special contribution, it is doubtful that Miss Liberty would be standing today. His design for her interior support called for a strong center pylon of four iron girders rising from the base to her neck. It would be the world's tallest iron structure at that time. From this "backbone" radiated a skeleton of smaller beams connected by thin spring-like rods to a webbing of iron straps lining the inside of the statue's copper skin.

Thus Liberty's skin actually "floats" at the ends of these hundreds of spring-like rods giving it a flexibility that allows it to flex with temperature changes and the tremendous buffeting of harbor winds.

Separately, the thin copper skin and the lacy metal interior support would disintegrate in the screaming winter gales that howl around her. But joined together they form a strength far greater than the sum total of their individual parts.

Forerunner of the Skyscraper

Not only did this unique design presage aeronautical engineering involving fuselages and wings, but it prophesied modern skyscraper construction. The formed copper sheets of Liberty do not support each other's weight but are suspended by interior support, just as a skyscraper's exterior walls are hung on steel framework.

Another problem that Eiffel faced was Liberty's torch arm which soared over forty feet at a precarious angle. Again his ingenuity came to the fore when he designed a separate inner armature extending the length of the arm which branched from the main pylon's "shoulder." Strong and resilient, it allows the arm to sway in heavy winds which, though safe, can be disconcerting to someone up there changing her torch lights.

Finally, after four years' work, the some 300 completed copper pieces were taken out of the cavernous workshop to be temporarily assembled next door in the open. Levi P. Morton, America's minister to France, drove the first ceremonial copper rivet in her foot on October 24, 1881, and by the following year Parisians began craning their necks to gaze up at the massive collosus soaring above their tallest buildings.

By 1884—almost seven years in building—with her head and torch arm returned to Paris, she was finally completed. With scaffolding still reaching to her shoulders like a strange robe made of lace squares, she gazed serenely across the tiled rooftops of Paris.

The statue begins to go up.

A Sad Passing

However, there was one who did not get to see her fully formed, the one who inspired her creation: Edouard de Laboulaye.

The great statesman had died peacefully at his home on May 25, 1883, at the age of seventy-two. However, he had had a good view of what he so aptly called "a body of iron, a soul of fire," would look like as it neared completion on the rue de Chazelles. As one writer noted: "Did not Laboulaye, the America-worshiper,

Construction is well underway in this third picture of the sequence.

seem like a new Moses barred from entering the Promised Land and merely shown his work on the point of fruition?"

A new Moses or not, he was hailed on both sides of the Atlantic for his "noble and unselfish motives."

As the American minister, Levi Morton, said in his dispatch to the U.S. State Department: "He was a devoted friend to our country and our Government; although he had never crossed the ocean, he knew America and American history, I dare say, better than most Americans."

Laboulaye's presence was undoubtedly felt at the banquet held on May 21, 1884, celebrating Liberty's completion.

The one in whose honor the banquet was held was probably the closest of all to Laboulaye, his long-time friend Frédéric Bartholdi. Joining him at the festive table was Ferdinand de Lesseps, the famed engineer of the Suez Canal, who had succeeded Laboulaye as president of the *Union Franco-Americaine*.

Meeting the Mother

Another of the many French and American guests at the banquet was French Senator Jules Francois Jennottee-Bozerian, who took the opportunity in his after-dinner speech to relate an anecdote revealing something about the guest of honor.

"On the day that I, with many others, first harnessed myself to the success of our work, which is now reaching its happy conclusion, Monsieur Bartholdi said to me, 'Come with me to the opera. You will understand later the special reason for my invitation.' I accepted. We entered a stage box, in a corner of which sat a lady of imposing appearance. Finding myself near Bartholdi, I said to him, 'That is the statue of Liberty Enlightening the World.' He pressed my hand, saying: 'Yes, it is.' "

The senator looked around the banquet table, smiling, and continued. "Do you know who that lady was? It was Bartholdi's mother!"

Cheers exploded.

"Was I right in telling you, gentlemen," he continued, "that while describing his many qualities, an important one had been forgotten, that of a son?"

More cheers rose, shimmering the crystal goblets on the table.

"You will join me, I am sure," he said, raising his glass, "in drinking a toast to Monsieur Bartholdi's filial piety!"

Shining Like a New Penny

Six weeks later on July 4, 1884, another celebration took place as a riot of fluttering red, white, and blue colors filled the outdoor foundry yard around the huge workshop of Gaget, Gautheir et Cie. This was the day of final ceremonies presenting Liberty to the United States. As some two hundred people stood at the foot of the towering statue, gleaming with the shine of a newly-minted penny, Ferdinand de Lesseps presented it to the United States "in the name of the French people."

Levi Morton, U.S. Minister to France, gravely received it "in the name of the American people."

"To you, *monsieur le ministre*," concluded de Lesseps in his presentation speech, "we now transfer this great statue and trust that it may forever stand as the pledge of friendship between France and the great republic of the United States."

"God Grant That It May Stand"

Morton, clearing his throat and squinting in the sun, read a telegram of congratulations from the president of the United States, Chester A. Arthur, which praised Bartholdi along with others and graciously thanked the people of France. Then, the minister ended with a prayer: "God grant that it may stand until the end of time, as an emblem of imperishable sympathy and affection between the Republics of France and the United States."

If Laboulaye had been there to hear the speeches, his heart would have thrilled at the use of "Republic" in connection with his beloved France and the country across the Atlantic that he also loved.

When the parchment deed in its gold case was officially handed over, a band played the rousing anthems of "The Marseillaise," "The Star Spangled Banner," and "Hail Columbia." Miss Liberty now belonged to the United States.

For some months the statue remained standing in Paris as it was felt that shipping it across the Atlantic during the winter was too dangerous. Then in the spring workmen began carefully dismantling it, numbering and packing the copper and iron sections in 210 wooden shipping crates.

Filling an Empty Place

The empty place it left against the Parisian sky was especially noted by thoughtful American residents. To express their appreciation, they commissioned a smaller copy, one quarter the size of Liberty, and presented it to Paris. It was originally set up on the *Place des États-Unis*, then five years later it was moved to the *Ile des Cygnes* downstream from the Eiffel Tower where it was rededicated as a gift from the United States.

The original Liberty in her wooden packing cases and weighing 220 tons, of which the copper itself weighed 88 tons, was loaded aboard seventy freight cars and shipped to the French port of Rouen. There she was hoisted aboard a government steamship, the *Isere*, which sailed for New York on May 21, 1885.

If Miss Liberty could have known the prevalent attitude toward her in her adopting country, she would have stepped right off the ship and remained in France.

It was embarrassing but true. With all the fanfare of presenting Miss Liberty to America, she did not have a place to stand. For even as the *Isere*, heavy with her hallowed cargo, plowed through the Atlantic toward New York, the Americans had not yet completed her pedestal.

Nine years had passed since they had started raising money for it. But apathy had stalled the fund-raising campaign which Bartholdi had helped to initiate when he returned to the United States on his second visit in 1876.

But back then no one foresaw the problems that would arise in securing finances. Nor could anyone even dream of the indignities that Miss Liberty herself would suffer before she was allowed to step upon her pedestal.

7

A LADY PUT TO SHAME

Centennial!

For all was optimism in the grand celebration year of America's Centennial, and 1876 would be a memorably joyous year for Frédéric Bartholdi in particular. He had come to America with the French delegation to attend the Philadelphia Centennial exhibition where he saw his monumental fountain enthusiastically received and crowds lining up to climb Miss Liberty's forearm holding the torch.

He also proudly watched the dedication of his statue of Lafayette in Union Square in New York City where there never was any question about funding. The statue itself was a gift from his government to the American people, and the pedestal had been erected and paid for by the French residents of the city. His eyes misted as the heroic figure, presenting heart and sword to the thirteen colonies, was unveiled while a brass band blared the "Marseillaise" and cannons thundered.

But of all the accolades, honors, and expressions of gratitude heaped on Bartholdi during his second visit, nothing could match what happened to the forty-two-year-old bachelor near the end of it.

A Summer Romance

It started with the summer being so hot that on one Sunday alone in New York twenty-one of the horses pulling street cars dropped dead on the street. Bartholdi, ill from the heat, fled to cooler Montreal where he wired his old friend, John La Farge, of his predicament. Soon there was a knock on his hotel room door;

and when he opened it who should be smiling at him but Jeanne-Emilie Baheux de Puysieux, the thirty-six-year-old cousin of La Farge, whom he had met on his first visit to America.

Jeanne lived in Montreal and La Farge could think of no better medicine for his friend Bartholdi. As Bartholdi wrote his mother: "When she took my hand, it gave me a deep feeling of comfort." And then with the diplomacy of a son who knew how his mother would receive this news of a third person in their lives, he added, "I felt as if she had been sent by you, Mother. Though there is neither wealth, nor beauty, nor society connections, nor musical talents," he continued, "she has the most likeable features—a heart of gold which reflects itself on her face."

Bartholdi quickly recovered, and he and Jeanne-Emilie spent many idyllic days with the La Farges in their beach house in Newport where they were married on December 20.

A new wife did not prevent him from continuing every effort to get the pedestal campaign fund under way. A month later, in January 1877, the *American Committee on the Statue of Liberty* was formed. Some of its prominent members included John Jay, William Evarts, and Theodore Roosevelt whose son, nicknamed "The Rough Rider," would become president of the United States.

When Bartholdi and his bride returned to France a month later, he felt that his "daughter," Miss Liberty, was in good hands, especially when he heard that on February 22, 1877, the United States Congress officially accepted her into the American family. As one of his countrymen, Charles Lefebre, put it: "...full of this contagious ardor and confidence in success which only a strong faith can give, he finally got others to share his idea...one will never know all that it cost him in efforts, in negotiations, and thankless work."

Lefebre had not exaggerated about what the statue had cost Bartholdi for he benefited little, if at all, from it monetarily. Thus one can well understand how his heart must have been grieved when he heard of the difficulties the pedestal fund-raising was meeting.

Rough Words

The cost of the pedestal had been estimated at $125,000, and even before Bartholdi left America a New York *Times* editorial of January 1877 lashed out at the expense. The editorial ended:

If we are to have the Statue, we must subscribe at least 2,000,000 francs, besides finding oil for the torch and a fat woman for the right thumb nail. No true patriot can countenance any such expenditure for bronze females in the present state of finances, and hence, unless the Frenchmen change their minds and pay for the Statue themselves, we shall have to do without it.

Metropolitan Combat

Philadelphia pricked its ears at this comment; and four days later at a dinner honoring Bartholdi, his old friend Colonel Forney toasted him and declared, "The city of Philadelphia would leap at the opportunity to get possession of it."

Responding like a wounded lion, the New York *Times* roared its reply, charging that Philadelphia had

> just shown an unmistakable intention of assuming the active duties of piracy [and it was] necessary that their nefarious intentions should be fully exposed...and thus, if possible, thwarted....They determined to seize upon a New York lighthouse* and set it up in the Delaware River, where it could guide the midnight eel-fisher and the belated muskrat to their respective homes....They must be told that their perverted desire can never be gratified. A limit must be put to their presumption, and it is well to draw the line at the lighthouse.

Irate as the *Times* was at Philadelphia's presumptuousness, it still had no concrete proposal to offer about raising funds. And though New Yorkers were becoming increasingly excited about it, using its form in patriotic party decorations and July 4th celebrations, the average person felt it was up to the wealthy to come up with the money.

And though the United States Congress had approved Bedloe's Island as the site, it refused to appropriate any funds for the pedestal and erection.

Hoping for a Miracle

Even so, the American Committee, hoping against hope that a miracle would happen, went ahead with plans for the pedestal. It would be built in the middle of old Fort Wood which once protected the city from any enemy ship steaming through the Narrows. The fort's massive outside walls, which formed an eleven-pointed star, would form a perfect base, it was felt.

Lighthouse was a popular term applied to Miss Liberty, as it was commonly assumed this to be the role she would fill. Perhaps it stemmed from Bartholdi's original plan to have light streaming from the diadem windows under her crown. There was no thought then of an illuminated torch which was designed as a frozen flame of copper.

Drawing of a proposal for the pedestal project by Bartholdi c.1880. From the Musée Bartholdi, Colmar.

But what would be the best shape for the pedestal? Bartholdi knew it had to be aesthetically pleasing, big enough to solidly support the towering statue, yet simple enough to allow the statue to remain the focus of attention.

Several designs were offered, one of them Bartholdi's own. His showed a stepped pyramid pedestal which looks very much like the pyramid on the great seal of the United States (seen on dollar bills). The pyramid has thirteen levels signifying the original colonies, above which is the "Eye of God" radiating spiritual light.

However, it was felt this presented too much of a mass, and in 1881 a well-known American architect was finally selected. Bartholdi's heart undoubtedly warmed at the announcement, for he had met the architect on his first visit to the United States in 1871, in the company of his old friend John La Farge in Newport.

A Unique Architect

He was Richard Morris Hunt. But more than previous acquaintance was undoubtedly the cause of Bartholdi's enthusiasm. For the architect who would design his statue's pedestal had already carved his own niche in history by having achieved several famous firsts.

Moreover, their two careers had worked in dramatic concert with each other. Each had left his homeland to travel to the other's country to contribute to its architectural skyline. And Bartholdi could not help but see in Hunt his counterpart in French-American relations. For Hunt had gone to Paris not only to study, but to contribute of his talent in creating some of France's most monumental buildings.

What could be more fitting than for one to create the pedestal on which the other's monument would stand?

Richard Hunt, architect to the wealthy and designer of the Statue of Liberty's pedestal. From *Harper's Weekly*, July 12, 1884.

An American in Paris

Richard Morris Hunt was born in Vermont in 1827, long before any established schools of architecture existed in the United States. When he was sixteen his mother took him and his brother William (later to become a famous painter) to Paris where Richard studied under a well-known architect, Hector Lefuel. When he was nineteen Richard enrolled in the famed *Ecole des Beaux Arts*, becoming the first of many American architects to study there. He stayed on in Paris where he was placed in charge of constructing an addition to the famed Louvre, the *Pavillon de la Bibliothéque*. As one contemporary architect noted: "There is a certain picturesque surprise in the spectacle of a Yankee lad giving form and character to one of the imperial monuments of France."

Though a promising career and fortune awaited him in France, Hunt felt that his real future lay in America. He returned at the age of twenty-seven to his homeland where he earned fame as a leader in the American Renaissance of architecture. Besides building the Astor Library and the new facade of the Metropolitan Museum of New York, he helped construct the dome of our nation's

Capitol in Washington and went on to create many illustrious mansions such as the famed Vanderbilt "Biltmore" estate near Asheville, North Carolina, and the "Breakers" in Newport, Rhode Island.

Hunt was also a distinguished founder of the American Institute of Architects. But perhaps his most important contribution was his role in establishing the first architectural school in America. Before his time no American university thought the field worth teaching. Hunt, however, had collected a considerable library on architecture and was a natural teacher. When several young men pleaded with him to take them as students, he obliged. One of them, William R. Ware, later became a founder of Columbia University's School of Architecture, the very first institution of its kind in the United States.

Classic Grandeur

In designing the pedestal of the Statue of Liberty, Richard Morris Hunt dedicated his skill and talent in combining grandeur with classic tradition. The eighty-nine-foot-high pedestal—almost nine stories tall—was designed to direct the eye to the statue. Pleasing in appearance and simple in form of reinforced concrete with textured granite facing and Doric columns, its forty shields lining the base represented the number of states then in the Union. The amount of concrete used in the base would be the world's largest concrete pour yet.

Huge steel beams anchored within it would lock into Eiffel's iron core of the statue. So strong and solid had Hunt designed it that it was said that to turn the statue over, one would have to turn the whole island over with it.

The cornerstone of all this—a six-ton block of Connecticut granite—was laid on August 5, 1884, one month after the July 4 presentation of Miss Liberty by France to the United States. The ceremony itself reflected the apathy regarding the pedestal. Of the 750 invitations sent by the American Committee to prominent people, many were turned down with regret, the usual excuse being that they would be out-of-town for the summer.

Not long after the cornerstone was laid, work stopped altogether on the pedestal for lack of funds. Part of the problem was unexpected expenses in excavating the heavy masonry of the fort.

Ridicule and Indignity

Heaped on top of the apathy was ridicule from a number of sources. One newspaper, under the title of "Looking a Gift Horse in the Mouth," wrote:

> The painful parsimony of the Frenchmen who have undertaken to present this city with the statue of "Liberty Enlightening the World" is simply disgusting. They have, in effect, told us that we cannot have the statue unless we provide it with a pedestal. This effort to compel us to pay out of our own money for the embellishment of our harbor has not yet been condemned by the press with the severity it deserves.

The writer then recommended that the French people put up the statue and pay $10,000 to the United States as rent for its location.

Laying of the pedestal's cornerstone, with placement of the time capsule. From *Harper's Weekly*, Aug. 16, 1884.

A congressman stated that it was unseemly for the United States to be represented by a woman in this prestigious location and that in its place a statue of Uncle Sam should be erected.

And though no businessmen had, as yet, come up with any substantial donations, one did offer to contribute $25,000. His stipulation: that the name of his product—Castoria—be displayed on the pedestal for one year.

The Fight Goes On

But again, when other cities indicated interest in Miss Liberty, New Yorkers bristled. When Boston offered a site, the New York *Times*, referring to "the latest stab," thundered:

> This statue is dear to us...and no third-rate town is going to step in and take it from us. Philadelphia tried that in 1876, and failed. Let Boston be warned in time that she can't have our Liberty. We have more than a million people in this city who are resolved that the great lighthouse statue shall be smashed into minute fragments before it shall be stuck up in Boston harbor.

"But, we need not lose it," continued the *Times* in great harumph, calling for fund-raising action. "No doubt the Committee...will now bestir themselves."

And "bestir themselves" they did, remounting a massive campaign with "An Appeal to the People of the United States" and hiring a public relations expert, Mahlon Chance, to canvass the nation.

But the program met lukewarm response. Others felt that since the statue would be in New York's harbor, why shouldn't New Yorkers pay for it?

In addition to all this, Miss Liberty began drawing fire from some Protestants and Catholics as being "pagan and idolatrous." John Gilmory Shea, in his printed article entitled "Our Great Goddess and Her Coming Idol," worried

> ere long the idol of the goddess "Liberty Enlightening the World" will be set up on Bedloe's Island, doubtless as was Nabuchodonosor's [sic] great statue of old, with sound of harp and sackbut and psaltery, and woe will betide the man who does not at the sound fall down and worship.

Misunderstood Theology

In referring to the ancient Roman goddesses of liberty, he added in sarcasm that

Some antiquated persons with medieval ideas may choose to believe in One Who proclaimed His doctrine eighteen centuries ago in Palestine and look up to Him as "the true Light that enlighteneth the world," and believe that men can be really free only "with the freedom wherewith He hath made us free" but as their voices are not likely to be heard amidst the general joy, and the shouting, and the music, we may in advance enter our protest.

It wasn't, however, misunderstood theology among a small representation of religious leaders that threatened the establishment of Miss Liberty on American soil; it continued to be the plain old garden variety of apathy.

In March 1885, eight years after the fund-raising campaign began and with the completed statue due to arrive in New York harbor within three months, only fifteen feet of the eighty-nine-foot pedestal existed. Red-faced members of the American Committee sat down and chewed their pencils. At least $100,000 was needed, an astronomical figure to them. They issued a desperate appeal:

> If the money is not forthcoming the statue must return to its donors to the everlasting disgrace of the American people, or it must go to some other city to the everlasting disgrace of New York. Citizens...we ask you once and for all to prevent so painful and humiliating a catastrophe.

The Man Nobody Wanted

One New Yorker who had followed the campaign with keen interest was an American immigrant who knew only too well the pain of rejection and humiliation. Joseph Pulitzer was born in Mako, Hungary, in 1847, son of a Jewish grain dealer and a Catholic Austro-German mother. At age seventeen he tried to enlist in his own Austrian emperor's army. He was rejected because of weak eyes and an "unpromising physique."

No doubt about the latter. The teen-ager could have modeled for Ichabod Crane. Six foot tall, he was all skin and bones with an "unpromising physique" highlighted by a large nose, a prominent chin, and an Adam's apple.

The chin reflected a strong will; turning his back on Austria, he volunteered for the French army offering to fight overseas. Rejected again, he applied to the British expeditionary forces which desperately needed men in India. Turned down for the third time, he went to Hamburg to find work on sailing ships. Instead, he met an agent recruiting for the Union Army in America's Civil War. Finally, someone wanted him. He eagerly signed up, was shipped

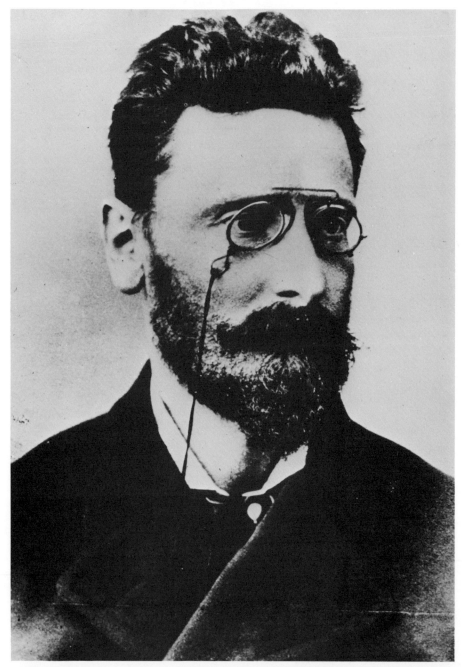

Joseph Pulitzer, the newspaper publisher whose support was crucial to the fundraising for the statue's pedestal.

to New York, and went right into service. The lanky, skinny private's ardor for army life was soon quenched by a war that he later found "a vague memory of torture." He was eventually mustered out with a fierce hatred of injustice, intolerance, ignorance, and malice.

He took a reporter's job with a German newspaper in St. Louis and, at age twenty-two, a strong sympathizer with the underdog, entered Missouri politics and was elected to the state legislature. In 1878 he bought the bankrupt St. Louis *Dispatch* for $2,500, merged it with the tottering *Post* and launched a circulation drive with eye-catching news features. By 1883 he had gone to New York, where for $346,000 he bought the *World*, a failing newspaper operated by robber baron Jay Gould.

A Man for All Seasons

According to W.A. Swanberg's biography, "Pulitzer's ideal was a newspaper so astonishingly liberal, reformist and newsy that it would charm the workmen and still appeal to a segment of the white-collar class."

With an understanding eye, he went after the readership of immigrants flooding into New York. He gave them an attractive paper, interesting, and grounded in the ideals of freedom that had brought them to America. In a year the *World* had leaped ahead of almost every other New York paper in circulation.

Perhaps it was Joseph Pulitzer's memory of the day his ship sailed into New York harbor bringing him to a new life. Or perhaps he was rankled by the wealthy people who ignored Miss Liberty's need. Whatever, he was challenged. In March 1885 he launched a campaign that made newspaper history. The substance of his editorial read:

> It would be an irrevocable disgrace to New York City and the American Republic to have France send us this special gift without our having provided even so much as a landing place for it...there is but one thing that can be done. We must raise the money.

> The *World* is the people's paper, and it now appeals to the people to come forward and raise this money. The $250,000 that the statue had cost was paid in by the masses of the French people—by the workingmen, the tradesmen, the shop girls, the artisans—by all, irrespective of class or condition. Let us respond in like manner. Let us not wait for the millionaires to give this money. It is not a gift from the millionaires of France to the millionaires of America but a gift of the whole people of France to the whole people of America.

> Take this appeal to yourself personally...give...something...however little...let us hear from the people.

Within one week readers had responded with over $2,000, to which the *World* added $1,000 from its own coffers. And now the paper began receiving wonderful copy for its continuing campaign through such letters as this:

> Please receive from two little boys one dollar for the pedestal. It is our savings. We give it freely.

I am a wee bit of a girl, yet I am ever so glad that I was born in time to contribute my mite to the pedestal fund. When I am old enough I will ask my papa and mamma to take me to see the statue, and I will always be proud that I began my career by sending you $1.00 to aid in so good a cause.

Enclosed please find five cents as a poor office boy's mite.

Mail brought a dollar from "a party of poor artists," and another from a "young man of foreign birth who had seen enough of monarchial governments to appreciate the blessing of this Republic."

There was $7.25 from "a few poor fellows whose pockets are not as deep as a well but whose love of Liberty is wider than a church door.... May heaven help your good work; it seems that New York's rich men don't."

Children's Pennies

Envelopes with pennies and bills poured in from not only New York and the surrounding states but from as far away as Texas and Minnesota. Money came from shop girls, factory workers, actors, physicians, farmers. And always there were childish scrawls: "I am a little girl nine years old and I will send you a pair of my pet game bantams if you will sell them and give the money to the Statue." And "We send you $1.00, the money we have saved to go to the circus."

As contributions from the little people, the common people, flooded in, there were those who could not help but be reminded of the apostle Paul's words: "But God has chosen the foolish things of the world to put to shame the wise, and God has chosen the weak things of the world to put to shame the things which are mighty" (1 Cor. 1:27).

In a little over a month some 120,000 contributions—mostly in small amounts—flooded the offices of Pulitzer's paper.

Other newspapers chimed in and contributions began pouring in from other parts of the United States as well. The Philadelphia *Daily News* stated that the Statue of Liberty did not belong to New York but to the whole country.

Churches had something to say. The North Baptist Church in Philadelphia reported that they would take a special collection on Sunday, May 31, 1885. The minister, Reverend H.H. Barbour suggested that Decoration Day for other churches would be "a particularly appropriate occasion to appreciate liberty which enables people to worship in perfect freedom."

Others did follow suit, including synagogues; the children's classes of one sent in their collection of $16.88.

On Its Way!

With funds flowing in, the American Committee happily announced that work on the pedestal was underway, and contributions accelerated. Immigrants responded in droves, like the man who wrote:

> I received today my first earnings and I am able to spare ten percent of it for Liberty's sake. I would send you more if I could, as I know how to appreciate Liberty because I am a Jew who emigrated from Russia to this city a few years ago. I think that the Germans who

Construction work on the statue's foundation mass on Bedloe's Island, New York. From *Harper's Weekly*, July 12, 1884.

fled in 1848 to this country and the Jews who came here a few years ago from such countries where they have been persecuted...ought to support you in your noble undertaking.

Other ethnic groups joined in, including an appeal to support the campaign in the *IL Progresso Italo-Americano* in New York City.

Businesses began contributing, including the American Express Company, and a $2,000 check came in from the Amateur Minstrel Jubilee at the Academy in New York.

It now appeared that everyone—man, woman, and child—wanted to come to the rescue of Miss Liberty. Special theatrical performances, athletic activities, and dances were held. Miniature copies of the statue were sold. And the *World* enthusiastically continued its campaign: "Gather in the money dollar by dollar, dime by dime, penny by penny!"

> Stone by stone, no more to stop,
> Freedom's throne is builded up;
> Upward goes the granite gray,
> Still it grows with every day.
> Still they come like drops of rain,
> Every sum a welcome gain;
> Roll the ball, and still it grows,
> One and all—and up she goes!

In the meantime the *Isere* had steamed into New York on June 17, 1885, where she was met by the French North Atlantic Squadron and escorted into port under flying colors. Two days later as a brisk wind snapped the United States and French flags on a tug, gently swaying in the harbor, Commandant de Saune of the *Isere* officially conveyed the statue from France to America.

The elderly man with the silver goatee and handlebar mustache, who accepted the title deeds on behalf of the United States, represents one of the most tragic and most inspiring stories in the annals of our country's history.

As the brass band's notes lifted with the harbor wind, it was an emotional moment for the elderly man who had the honor of representing his country in this historic ceremony.

He had earned it. For he was General Charles P. Stone, chief engineer, who had been in charge of constructing the pedestal since the ground-breaking and would help oversee the erection of the statue herself. Yet, even then few remembered his story, his anguished struggle for truth, justice, and liberty personified by the statue whose title deeds he was then accepting.

As military salutes were smartly exchanged and national anthems played, his mind undoubtedly traveled twenty-three years back to the time when he was arrested as a traitor to the United States. In fact, across the sparkling harbor waters was the very U.S. Army fort where he had been imprisoned.

8

A MAN PUT TO SHAME

A Promising Leader

It all began in the early days of the Civil War. Then a man in his thirties, Brigadier General Stone, a West Point graduate, was one of his country's most promising military leaders. The gentle-eyed man had earlier distinguished himself in the Mexican War, then entered civilian life as a construction engineer. When the Civil War began he rejoined the army as Inspector General of the District of Columbia, where his main responsibility was guarding the life of President Lincoln. The president trusted him and he soon became a brigadier general heading a division of volunteers under General George McClellan, Commander of the Army of the Potomac.

In the fall of 1861 Stone was ordered by McClellan to make a reconnaissance of an area near Leesburg, Virginia, some forty-five miles northwest of Washington. Just west of the Potomac River, it turned out to be a Confederate stronghold. Stone had sent over two regiments which occupied the wooded heights called Ball's Bluff. When the Southerners attacked, the Union forces suffered a devastating defeat with many killed, including their unseasoned commander, Edward Baker, a popular and flamboyant colonel who also had served as a senator from Oregon.

Though it was a small battle compared to those that would come later, the defeat loomed gargantuan in the eyes of the press and the nation.

Scapegoat

Someone had to be the scapegoat.

General Stone had earlier incurred the wrath of several politicians whom he had castigated for interfering in army affairs. Now he became the target of vicious and false rumors. Campfire gossip making the rounds in Washington had it that he had collaborated with the enemy, that he had actually sent his troops into a trap on Ball's Bluff.

At the same time radicals in Congress, who felt that the Union forces lacked aggressiveness, created a committee to investigate General McClellan and the Army of the Potomac. Its chairman, Senator "Bluff Ben" Wade, ruthless and unscrupulous, quickly swung the committee's gun-sights on General Stone.

Stone was hauled up before the committee and, without being allowed any real opportunity to defend himself, he was railroaded into being arrested for treason.

"I have, so help me heaven, but one object," he cried, "to see the United States successful." Despite his pleas and the lack of evidence, the general was hustled to Fort Lafayette in New York harbor where he was thrown into solitary confinement. After fifty days in the dungeon, his health had failed so badly that he was moved to nearby Fort Hamilton. Still intensely loyal to his country, the aggrieved Stone begged for an official trial so that his record could be cleared. Finally, in August 1862, after six month's imprisonment, he was released; but he was given no official vindication nor military assignment. For months he made the rounds of officials, including Lincoln and Stanton, pleading to have his name cleared. All sympathized with him and condemned his harsh treatment, but none, perhaps because of the press of war, took steps to help him.

Under a Cloud

In February 1863 he finally won an acquittal, but his name was still under a cloud as no official order had been issued to clear him. Later he was given command of a brigade in the Army of the Potomac. Before leaving for the spring battles in 1864, he made a final plea to the president:

> This will be the last letter which I shall address to you during my life, or to justify myself in history.... I respectfully ask, for the sake of the service which I have loved and never dishonored, and for the sake of my name in history...that some act, some word, some order may issue...which shall place my name clear of reproach, as I know it should be.

General Charles P. Stone, engineer of the pedestal. From *Harper's Weekly*, July 12, 1884.

That act, that order, never came.

After the war he resigned his commission, and his engineering skill earned him work with mining and construction companies. In 1870 he went overseas where he became chief of staff of the Army of Egypt.

Back in the United States, many remembered the courage of this dignified man who had fought so desperately against such tragic odds. When he returned to his homeland in 1883, they also remembered his skills as an engineer. And when it came time that

The pedestal as designed by Hunt.

year to select an engineer who would make certain that the pedestal of the Statue of Liberty was constructed well, the Monument Committee could think of no finer man than General Charles P. Stone. He was also invited to join the Monument Committee along with such dignitaries as Bartholdi and Pulitzer.

The names of those who had maligned this gentle-eyed man have long since been forgotten. But General Charles P. Stone will always be remembered in connection with the world-renowned symbol of the liberty for which he fought so dearly. As the Bible says: "So I will restore to you the years that the swarming locust has eaten" (Joel 2:25).

After the statue's title deeds were accepted by General Stone, the officers and crew of the *Isere* were taken to shore and enthusiastically welcomed by a parade through the city and another ceremony at City Hall.

On June 22 the crates began to be unloaded on Bedloe's Island and stored at the base of the pedestal, which was now being constructed as fast as possible.

In the meantime contributions continued to roll in. One of the last received was fifty cents from ten people who had attended Ulysses S. Grant's funeral in August 1885, and instead of taking the streetcar home, they walked, sending in the money they saved from carfare.

On August 11, 1885, the *World* proudly announced in headline banners:

ONE HUNDRED THOUSAND DOLLARS
TRIUMPHANT COMPLETION OF THE *WORLD'S* FUND
FOR THE LIBERTY PEDESTAL

> Ah, Madame Liberty, God bless you!
> Since all the cash is there at hand,
> No longer need it now distress you
> The question of a place to stand.
>
> Soon you in your allotted station,
> Firm in your tower, strong and tall,
> Will give this truth a new illustration
>
> THE PEOPLE ARE THE ALL IN ALL.

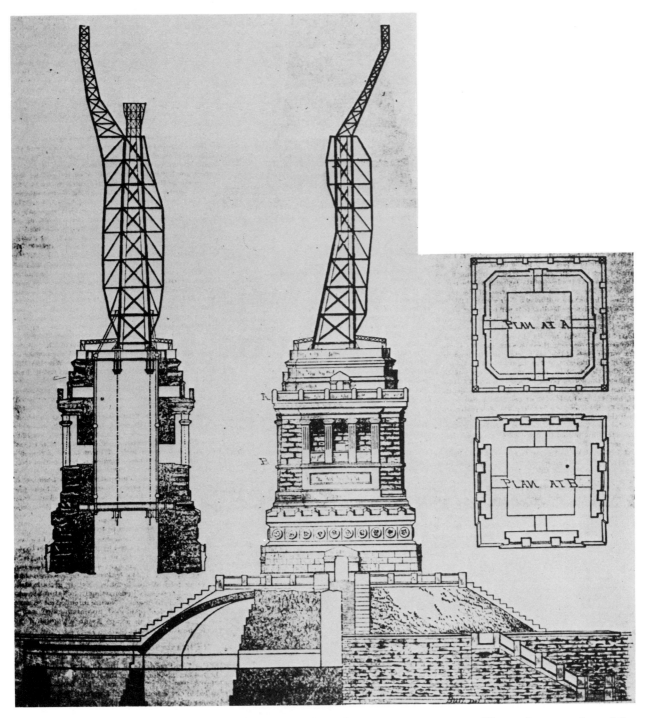

Plans and cross-sections of the statue's armature and pedestal. From *Scientific American*, 1885.

Everyone, it seems, benefitted from Joseph Pulitzer's newspaper campaign. Miss Liberty herself, Americans who became united in one common cause, and the *World* which had boosted its circulation to 150,000 copies, seven times what it was at the beginning of the campaign.

The pedestal was finally completed in the spring of 1886. At the ceremony held on April 22, Chief Engineer Stone happily an-

Reconstruction of the statue in New York.

nounced that not a man had been killed or injured during the construction.

Then the assembly of the statue began. First rose Eiffel's ingenious iron pylon and framework, a lacy monolith against the harbor sky. Then, on a hot July 12, another ceremony celebrated the attachment to the frame of the first two copper sections—dubbed "Bartholdi and Pulitzer."

The assembly of Miss Liberty was not as easy as expected. Some of the larger curved copper sheets that had been formed in

Paris had flattened out somewhat in the crates, and it took some time to re-form them.

Also, the identifying numbers had come off some of the sections and others had been mislabeled. As Miss Liberty began to assume her dimensions it became difficult at times to find and fit the proper pieces together. Sometimes it was like finding the right piece to a jigsaw puzzle, with men hoisting two and even three pieces by derrick to determine the correct one. And, unlike the easy-to-work-from scaffolding that assemblers had used in Paris, the men on Bedloe's Island used steeplejack methods—planks sus-

Artisans at work in the statue's interior in New York Harbor. Wood engraving from *Frank Leslie's Illustrated Newspaper,* Oct. 9, 1886.

pended on cables—as they riveted the copper sections together.

In October 1886 Miss Liberty was completely formed except for the sole of her right foot. This section, about nine-by-four feet in size, was left off to allow workmen entry into the statue. From a distance they resembled ants crawling in and out of her sandal. Finally, this last piece was riveted into place.

Miss Liberty was complete. She had stepped across the Atlantic and now stood on the site where her sculptor first envisioned her fifteen years previously.

October 28, 1886, was set for her unveiling. It would be a day full of surprises, mistakes, protests, and wonderful excitement.

It had to be a deeply emotional moment for Frédéric Bartholdi that October 25, 1886, when his ship, *La Bretagne*, steamed into New York harbor. For the first time he would see his "daughter" standing in reality where he had so excitedly envisioned her fifteen years earlier on his initial trip to America.

One can picture him standing on the breeze-swept deck straining for a glimpse of his creation as the harbor expanded before him. And then...his hands tighten on the rail and his throat tightens as in the distance he sees her, almost as if she were striding toward him in greeting.

"I am much pleased," he said later to reporters surrounding him on Bedloe's Island where he examined Miss Liberty at close hand. "It is a grand sight." He looked up thoughtfully at the towering figure, copper gleaming in the sun. "I was worried about some of the lines." He nodded his head. "It is a success."

After walking about the island with his wife, Jeanne, and fellow members of the accompanying French delegation, he added: "The dream of my life is accomplished; I see the symbol of unity and friendship between two nations—two great republics."

Turning to his companion, Ferdinand de Lesseps, the great canal builder, he said: "It is a consolation to know that this statue will exist thousands of years from now, long after our names shall have been forgotten."*

But judging from all indications during the hectic days surrounding the October 28 dedication, the name Bartholdi would shine forever. Presented golden keys to the city by Mayor Grace and feted at Delmonico's, he saw his portrait being hawked by street vendors and heard the words "Bartholdi Day" as much as "Liberty Day."

He awakened early on the day of dedication, Thursday, October 28, to a gray dawn. And though a gentle rain began to fall about nine o'clock in the morning, it did not stop thousands of parade goers from lining Fifth Avenue, many balancing on boxes and stools for a better view.

They saw twenty thousand soldiers, sailors, and war veterans following marching bands. There were floats and fire engines, brought up by college students and a multitude of clubs and organizations including the *Société Comarienne, Union Alsacienne,*

BAPTISM IN NEW YORK

---

*When Bartholdi died in 1904, he had never recovered the more than $20,000 which he had put into the statue, for he had neither requested nor received a commission for designing it. As any other artist would, he did "sign" it—if one were a steeplejack, he would find the signature, an initial "B" within one of the folds of her gown.

Gardes Rochambeau, and *Société Israelite* composed of Jewish people of French origin.

New York was a French city that day, aflutter with tricolor and its streets ringing with "The Marseillaise."

All twenty thousand paraders snapped to attention as they passed the reviewing stand in Madison Square Park where President Grover Cleveland, Bartholdi, and de Lesseps stood (for good reason; their chairs were awash with rain). Earlier, Bartholdi had been greeted by President Cleveland with the words: "You are the greatest man in America today!"

"Through your courtesy," bowed the diplomatic sculptor.

Even so, three little girls lent impact to the Chief Executive's pronouncement when they broke free of the parade and rushed up to the reviewing stand to present flowers which, they made emphatically clear, were only "for Mr. Bartholdi!"

Hardly had the last notes of the scarlet-coated Marine band conducted by John Philip Sousa sounded when the president and entourage boarded the USS *Despatch* on the Hudson at West Twenty-third Street. The small naval boat led a flotilla of three hundred excursion steamers, tugs, and yachts to Bedloe's Island where at anchor lay eight full-rigged American warships along with several French dreadnoughts. Jack-tars sprang into the rigging where they stood elbow to elbow on the yardarms in smart salute.

Below, naval cannons thundered in the twenty-one-gun Presidential Salute, as white smoke billowed into the mist further shrouding the statue from view.

No Ladies Allowed

Over three thousand people crowded the eleven-acre island waiting for the unveiling ceremonies set for 3:00 P.M. Practically all of them were men, for newspapers reported that no tickets would be issued to ladies, ostensibly for their protection, and "those who might try to slip through are warned that the crush will be great."

Reacting in true feminist fashion, the New York State Woman Suffrage Association chartered a boat to ply near the island from which members using megaphones would make acclamatory speeches praising Liberty embodied as a woman and "raising the hope of all women."

Even so, we know there were at least two women on the island—Bartholdi's wife and de Lesseps's little daughter, Tototte, who proudly clutched a "liberty rock" she had found near the base of the statue.

There were also many men who were not supposed to be there. It happened because the Arrangements Committee, by mistake, included tickets for Mayor Grace and his party with those for the Board of Aldermen, delivered to "Big Jim" Nooney, president of the City Council.

Nooney had his own ideas about who should get the tickets which, it is said, earned him even more admirers among the rank and file. But everyone who finally made it to the island did so with some risk, for the waters churned with thousands of gyrating craft from steamers to rowboats piloted by white-faced helmsmen frantically blowing whistles to avoid collisions.

Finally, with the president and other dignitaries, including the governor, Pulitzer, and Secretary of the Navy Whitney ensconced on the speaker's platform, the band's marathon music ceased and the ceremony began.

The Reverend Richard S. Storrs, a Brooklyn minister, gave the invocation concluding with the Lord's Prayer. As de Lesseps gave the presentation address, his silver mustache still crisp in the rain, the constant hooting of steam whistles from the harbor caused him to wryly note that "steam which has done so much good...is at present doing us harm." He finished by commenting on the Panama Canal which he planned to build (but would not finish), and then the crowd clamored for Bartholdi.

Jumping the Gun

He was not on the platform, however, for he was then perched within the head of Miss Liberty grasping a rope attached to a giant French flag covering her face. He was waiting for a signal from a young boy standing on the platform three hundred feet below who would wave a handkerchief when the next speaker, Senator William Evarts, had finished his address for the American Committee. Evarts began speaking and after completing the words "the indomitable will of the great sculptor Bartholdi," he paused for breath. The boy, thinking it the end of the speech, waved to Bartholdi and the tricolor slid away from Miss Liberty's face.

"Hail Liberty!" shouted someone on the platform, and the crowd broke into cheers. The vessels in the harbor picked up the enthusiasm and for fifteen minutes there was a constant hooting, booming, and howling of whistles from the deep bass of ocean ships to the shrill piping of launches.

Evarts, astonished and flustered, turned and finished reading his speech to those present. When all finally quieted down President Cleveland, in a clear, strong voice, gave probably one of the shortest and most cogent speeches of his career which, in part, said:

> We will not forget that Liberty has made here her home, nor shall her chosen altar be neglected. Willing votaries will constantly keep alive its fires and these shall gleam upon the shores of our sister Republic in the East. Reflected thence and joined with answering rays, a stream of light shall pierce the darkness of ignorance and man's oppression until Liberty enlightens the world.

Bartholdi's models for the statue found in his home in Colmar, France, after its liberation by Allied troops on February 3, 1945.

Silverwork trophy by Tiffany given to Bartholdi in 1886 by Pulitzer and his contributors to the pedestal project. Inscribed "All Homage and Thanks to the Great Sculptor, Bartholdi" and "A Tribute from the New York World and over 121,000 Americans to Auguste Bartholdi and The Great Liberty Loving People of France 1886." In the Musée Bartholdi, Colmar.

Other speeches followed along with music, and then the entire crowd sang the Doxology as the brass band played "Praise God from Whom All Blessings Flow." The Right Reverend Henry C. Potter, an Episcopalian from New York, pronounced the benediction, and then there was a mad scramble of three thousand people trying to get off the island at once.

It was over. *The Statue of Liberty Enlightening the World* had been properly baptized and now, as a full-fledged American citizen, she had been naturalized as would the millions of immigrants who would eventually pass by her, gazing up in awe and hopeful anticipation.

One person was not at the dedication, one who was probably as important as any in making a contribution to the statue. Instead she was ill in her room and few thought of her. But millions have heard of her since.

Her story is about a woman who found her way back to God.

SOUL OF A SONNET

Pressing the end of the pen to her chin, the teen-aged girl gazed thoughtfully for a moment out of the lead-paned window of her family's brownstone in lower Manhattan. Then, dipping the pen into a silver inkwell on the mahogany desk, she quickly wrote lines of lyric poetry on the thick vellum paper. It was 1866 and, at age seventeen, Emma Lazarus was already a published poet.

Her first book, *Poems and Translations*, had already merited the attention of William Cullen Bryant. Thrilled at this honor, Emma still remained a deeply sensitive and shy maiden who now dedicated herself even more single-mindedly to the calling to which she had felt led since the age of seven.

Through the house drifted sounds of laughter from her five sisters who were preparing for a cotillion to be held that evening. But Emma preferred to remain at home where she could indulge her brilliant and brooding soul in the extensive library collected by her father, Moses Lazarus, a prosperous sugar merchant.

A Romance of Words

Her lustrous eyes, soft olive-toned complexion, and classic features drew the eyes of many young scions. But Emma Lazarus's interest lay more in the romance of words than in dancing and sleigh rides through Central Park.

Thus she was drawn to the reigning poets of the day, especially to the Concord poet Ralph Waldo Emerson. She fastened on his philosophy of looking into one's own self to find a supporting faith: "Every man has his magnetic needle," he wrote, to be found "by trusting himself, by listening to the whisper of the voice within him."

Thrilled by his ideas, she responded: "To how many youthful hearts has not his word been the reason—nay more, the guiding star—that led them safely through periods of mental storm and struggle?"

Emerson's "trusting himself" became the guiding star of young Emma's early journey instead of the first and greatest commandment: *Thou shalt love thy God with all thy heart.* And as she sat impassively at her family's orthodox Passover table and heard the ancient words: "Let then each consider as though he himself had been delivered from Egypt," she had little concept of their import. For her family heritage of Spanish Jews meant little to her. After all, she was well aware of her own inborn inalienable rights; her future was her own.

"I Feel No Religious Fervor"

When her elderly teacher, Rabbi Gottheil, gently asked if she would write a poem for his Hebrew hymnbook, she answered: "I will gladly assist you as far as I am able; but that will not be much...I feel no religious fervor in my soul."

Instead, her fervor seemed inspired by the oracle of Concord when she met him at one of the rare parties she attended. In her journal she praised his "unforgettable eagle eyes, full of smiling wisdom." And when she sent him a copy of her book she was "astonished and delighted by the high estimate" he placed on it. He was also severe in his criticism, which she treasured; and the young poet placed her heart and soul into his hands, dedicating her second book, *Admetus and Other Poems*, "to my friend Ralph Waldo Emerson."

Emerson was the master; she would be his disciple. Inspired, she continued her writing, completing a novel about Goethe and the young maiden, Friederike Brion, who sat enamored at his feet.

Disappointment

Then the blow struck. Emerson published his anthology *Parnassus*, a collection of poems by contemporary writers. As Emma flipped through its pages she did not find any of her own in it. Her heart froze and she quickly sat down at her desk and penned a letter to Emerson expressing "extreme disappointment."

For weeks afterwards she watched the mail that daily filled the polished brass letter box on the Union Square brownstone, but there was no reply from the famous Concord poet.

Nothing could soothe her hurt, despite the fact that her new book *Alide* was drawing wide approval everywhere. Turgenev, in Paris, found it "sincere and poetical," and John Burroughs, in complimenting her, hoped that "you are not judging yourself so harshly....Cherish, encourage, insist upon yourself!"

But nothing could fill the void left by Emerson's silence. The twenty-five-year-old woman secluded herself more and more in the family mansion, now writing lines such as "I have not accomplished anything to stir, to awaken, to teach or suggest, nothing the world could not equally do without."

Sorrow

Then the deepest tragedy. Her mother, Esther, died, breaking a close protective circle. In attempting to console her, Edmund Stedman, an older banker who had earned a reputation as a poet, suggested that she consider the Jewish tradition as her artistic heritage. Again, Emma Lazarus shook her head. "I am proud of my blood and lineage," she replied, "but the Hebrew ideals do not appeal to me."

However, her heart quickened when, out of the blue, a letter arrived from Emerson who invited her to spend a week with him and his family in Concord. Ecstatic, she did so and loved the New England town which she found "lovely, smiling with its quiet slopes, quietest rivers." She also discovered something else. Perhaps it was the proximity, seeing someone close at hand for a while, for when Emma returned from Concord she left her enamorment of the Concord poet behind.

Instead she devoted herself to a childhood interest, Heinrich Heine, the renowned German poet of the early nineteenth century, and published her translation of his poems. As Heine was a Jew, her rabbi, Dr. Gottheil, asked why she didn't comment on Heine from a Jewish view; and again she turned away from the question.

At the same time others were turning away from thousands of Jews overseas who were dying horrible deaths because of their faith. A people easy to set apart, they became prey for demagogues seeking scapegoats. The infamous pogroms which began in Russia in 1879 swept into Bulgaria, Rumania, and other neighboring countries.

"These persecutions," cried the London *Times* in 1881, "have taken every form of atrocity in the experience of mankind....Men have been cruelly murdered, women brutally outraged, children dashed to pieces or burned alive in their homes."

The exodus of Jews fleeing persecution became the largest since the one led by Moses from Egypt, and ships filled with thousands of homeless exiles streamed into New York harbor. At that time there was no Ellis Island and the fugitives waited on Ward's Island in New York's East River, huddling in large government sheds.

When a group of women in Emma Lazarus's circle went to Ward's Island to see what help they could give, she accompanied them, probably rather diffidently, expecting to find "the great unwashed."

True, there were many of that category in the assemblage. But she was stunned by what she found among them. White-bearded men read from Latin and Greek texts, young students were able to discuss poetry in fluent English, gracious women spoke in cultured tones. She met "men of brilliant talents and accomplishments—the graduates of Russian universities, scholars of Greek as well as Hebrew, and familiar with all the principal European tongues—engaged in menial drudgery and burning with zeal in the cause of their wretched co-religionists."

Emma Lazarus's life was changed forever.

Revelation

As she faced her heritage, and her God, the ivory tower collapsed. Suddenly she felt herself at one with the people chosen to suffer. A great change came over Emma Lazarus at the age of thirty-three. Her prose and poetry became far superior to her work of the past, and her output soared. Once timid, fearful of argument, she plunged into heated public debate against prejudice with the skill of a veteran.

"Let us thank the Lord, Who made us those to suffer, not to do, this deed," became her battle cry. "Thank God," she exclaimed, "for having made the Jews the anvil, not the hammer, of oppression!" On fire with the spirit of God, she became a leader against inhumanity, fighting with her poetry.

"FREEDOM," she sang. "Freedom to love the law that Moses brought,/ To sing the songs of David and to think/ The thoughts Gabirol to Spinoza taught."

Jewish and Christian leaders rallied to her side as she arranged group meetings to aid the Eastern Jewish plight and joined in representations to the State Department in Washington, D.C.

God's divine promise became her burning concern. In her poem, "The New Ezekiel," she wrote:

> The Spirit is not dead; proclaim the word,
> Where lay dead bones, a host of armed men stand;
> I ope your graves, my people, saith the Lord,
> I shall place you living in your land.

At the age of thirty-four she visited England and Europe for the first time in her life. The trip enhanced her love for her native land, and she returned home in 1883 more enthused for the cause of freedom than ever.

Manuscript of "The New Colossus" as written by Emma Lazarus.

In the mound of letters waiting for her in the family brown-stone, she found one from William Evarts of the American Committee for the Statue of Liberty. The pedestal fund was in serious trouble; well-known writers and artists were invited to contribute work to be auctioned off.

Would Miss Lazarus help?

She was tired from the long trip and ill, more ill than she or anyone else then realized. Sighing, she sat down and penned her usual form of refusal: "I am not able to write to order."

However, she remembered Europe as it was, the imperialistic regimes, the division of classes, the ruined palaces with the stench of a dead past. Everything seemed to have some bearing on the figure she had seen pictured soon to rise on the bare rocks in New York harbor.

Two days after her refusal, she wrote a sonnet on "The New Colossus" and mailed it to Mr. Evarts. The committee called it "a beautiful poem which, it is hoped, will awaken to new enthusiasm the workers in our cause." It, along with other works, was published in a souvenir portfolio.

The sonnet, however, brought a relatively small amount at the auction, $1,500. And three years later when the Statue of Liberty was dedicated, Emma Lazarus, now very ill, was not present nor was her poem mentioned at the ceremonies. A year later, on November 19, 1887, she died of cancer at the age of thirty-eight and was buried in Brooklyn.

For six more years her poem was forgotten. Then, in 1903, Georgiana Schuyler, a sculptor, found a yellowed copy of the souvenir portfolio in a New York bookstore. Her heart was moved by the sonnet; she had it inscribed on a bronze tablet and with permission had it mounted on the second-floor landing inside the statue's base. Interestingly, the influx of immigrants to the United States exploded shortly after Emma Lazarus's poem was affixed to Miss Liberty's base. The annual average of immigrants arriving in America during the period of 1905 to 1914 was 1,012,194, compared to 462,879 during the period of 1895 to 1904.*

Emma Lazarus, whose inspiring poem has offered hope to millions.

*This was pointed out to the author by John Holbrook, Jr., architect and businessman, who has studied United States immigration figures in correlation with the Statue of Liberty. Besides the above information, he indicates the immigration into the United States began to increase significantly first after the launching of the statue project in 1875 and again after Miss Liberty's arrival in New York. John Holbrook feels that the strength of our nation has been in di-

A Soul of Fire

By 1945 the power of Emma Lazarus's message had become familiar to almost every American, and the bronze tablet was remounted next to Miss Liberty's main entrance where it is seen by 1.5 million visitors each year.

Bartholdi had given Miss Liberty a body of iron...Emma Lazarus had given her a soul of fire:

> Not like the brazen giant of Greek fame,
> With conquering limbs astride from land to land;
> Here at our sea-washed, sunset gates shall stand
> A mighty woman with a torch, whose flame
> Is the imprisoned lightning, and her name
> Mother of Exiles. From her beacon-hand
> Glows world-wide welcome; her mild eyes command
> The air-bridged harbor that twin cities frame.
>
> "Keep, ancient lands, your storied pomp!" cries she
> With silent lips. "Give me your tired, your poor,
> Your huddled masses yearning to breathe free,
> The wretched refuse of your teeming shore.
> Send these, the homeless, tempest-tost to me.
> I lift my lamp beside the golden door!"

rect ratio to our welcoming those fleeing persecution, poverty, and fear in their former lands, and points to the biblical admonition as the basis for this: "The stranger who dwells among you shall be to you as one born among you, and you shall love him as yourself; for you were strangers in the land of Egypt: I am the LORD your God" (Lev. 19:34). "And if one of your brethren becomes poor, and falls into poverty among you, then you shall help him; like a stranger or a sojourner that he may live with you" (Lev. 25:35).

Almost from the day that Miss Liberty took her stance in New York harbor, she became a being in her own right. In welcoming the "huddled masses" through the years, she has time and again defied man's attempts to manipulate and use her.

It has been so from the beginning. Her creators designed her as a gift with political overtones. As a nostalgic reminder of Lafayette and Rochambeau they hoped she would cement French-American relations. At the time it undoubtedly helped, but years later, who remembered? During World War II many American GIs in France were heard to complain: "They even claim they gave us the Statue of Liberty."

At her 1886 dedication she was seen as a symbol of America's fight for independence. Today most Americans think of Concord Bridge and the Liberty Bell in this respect.

Instead, the tall torchbearer in classic gown has become something uniquely her own, a personification of America.

She has become the cashier at the check-out counter, the worker on the auto assembly line, the farmer, the girl at the word processor, the carpenter, the miner, the husband, the mother.

She has become *us*.

When we look at her we see home, we see our cities and villages, our schools and town halls, our churches and synagogues.

"When I left here," said a soldier watching Liberty materialize in the mist as his ship returned from Europe, "that was just a statue. Now I know what it means."

A blind GI is helped to the rail by a buddy. "When we go by her," he says, "just tell me."

And another is heard to call: "Take down your torch, honey; I'm home!"

Much of this might be a heritage from our parents or grandparents.

FROM REVERENCE TO MALEVOLENCE

"She Wades in Water!"

Mela Neisner Lindsay of Denver, Colorado, remembers a chill, blustery morning in the spring of 1905, when "Our ship, a steamer of the German Bremen Line, anchored in New York harbor and I, as an immigrant child, saw the Statue of Liberty for the first time."

Descendants of the first German colonists who had settled in Russia during the reign of Catherine the Great, her family had fled the terrifying turmoil when Bolshevism began. After overcoming seemingly insurmountable odds, the little family boarded

ship in Hamburg and suffered eleven days and nights of seasick-
ness in overcrowded third class quarters shared with Jews, Hun-
garians, Serbians, Ukrainians, Poles, Austrians, and fellow
Russian-Germans.

Finally, when the ship dropped anchor in New York harbor:
"Papa brought Mama, my older sister, Lydia, and me up out of
the deep well of steerage into the daylight of a new world," she re-
calls.

"It was then that the statue lady looked down on me. My eyes
grew wide with wonder as Papa picked me up and held me over
the heads of the crowd on deck. I knew at once that she had recognized us, had even waited for us!

" 'Oh, Papa,' I cried, pointing into the swirling sea mist, 'the
goddess has waded into the water to meet us!'

" 'Ja, ja,' Papa spoke, his voice choking and holding me close

against his tear-stained cheek. 'Ja, *Liebchen*, in her land we hope to find a new life.' He swallowed, finding it difficult to speak.

" 'See,' he said, 'how even now, she holds high the torch and brings the book. Surely, this is the beauty of freedom and knowledge!'

"Extending his free arm to Mama and my sister, he pressed them forward. 'Look, my family,' he cried, 'so that you will see and always remember.'

"As we stood silent with Papa's strong arm around us, the morning sun broke through the mist and washed the sails of countless small ships with silver light.

"All around us people thrilled to the long awaited sight. Some sang songs of praise in strange tongues. Some wept for joy. Others remained silent, their eyes glistening with fierce hope.

"Papa put me down and stood at the ship's rail, lost in his own feelings. Then, he recited in a voice barely audible but from the depth of his soul, the words he knew were inscribed at the base of the statue. He had learned them over two years before when he first decided to come to America. Later, I memorized the words in my schoolroom in Kansas, where my family found new life as American farmers."

> Give me your tired, your poor,
> Your huddled masses yearning to breathe free....

A Universal Symbol

Because the Statue of Liberty has become so familiar a symbol of freedom through the years, men and women have attempted to use her in a thousand different ways. In World War I she was employed in Liberty Bond posters; some showed her draped in an American flag. "Remember Your First Thrill of American Liberty?" asked one poster, showing immigrants watching her from a ship's deck. "Your duty—Buy United States Government Bonds."

She has been used in trademarks, advertisements and, more and more, has been sharing Uncle Sam's job in posters and cartoons as a representative of our country. Her universal symbol for America was used in the movie *Planet of the Apes.* When the studio wanted the audience to quickly recognize a wasteland in the film as once being the site of the United States, it showed Liberty's head and arm protruding from the sands of an ocean beach.

And sometimes she has been taken advantage of.

In 1956 a husky blond man smashed his way through a locked door at the base of the statue's uplifted arm, scampered up it, and hung a Hungarian flag from the torch.

Nine years later a group of fanatics plotted to dynamite her arm. They almost succeeded. "If we could make the old girl blow her top, we'd really put a hurt on that old b——," said one extremist after his arrest.

Early in 1977 Iranian demonstrators took over the statue. They shattered seven glass windows in her crown and through it dropped a fifteen-foot-long banner screaming DOWN WITH THE SHAH. Then six of them sat inside the statue's head chained together. After a press conference in the crown which proved futile, they gave up and left.

And some incidents were humorous, as when a group of Puerto

Shipboard immigrants entering New York Harbor see the Statue of Liberty for the first time. Woodcut from *Frank Leslie's Illustrated Newspaper,* July 2, 1887.

Rican demonstrators surged into the statue's head and got into a shouting argument with a camera crew that was already there filming an Elliot Gould movie about a boxing kangaroo.

Most of the above demonstrations took place after Dave Moffitt, superintendent of the Statue of Liberty, moved onto the island with his family of wife, daughter, and two sons. Devout Lutherans, the Moffits became members of Manhattan's Gustavus Adolphus Church.

Interrupted Prayers

They were receiving Holy Communion there one Sunday when a call came telling Dave that Iranians had again chained themselves to the statue. They had dropped a 140-foot-long banner from the statue's crown proclaiming SHAH MUST BE TRIED AND PUNISHED. Dave Moffitt left the church and raced to the end of Manhattan where a staff boat rushed him to the island.

Within a few hours the demonstrators—seven Muslims—sat handcuffed in Dave's office, complaining about the Shah being allowed into America for gallbladder surgery. Then they asked to go outside and kneel toward Mecca.

"Fine," said Dave, but then he looked out and saw all the television cameramen waiting. Obviously the demonstrators had publicity on their minds, not prayers.

"I'm not going to give them all this free PR," he said to his staff. "We're just going to make them look like nice guys. And they're jerks."

Back in his office he told the demonstrators no.

"Why not?" they argued.

"Because you didn't let me finish my prayers."

But not all demonstrations involved people chaining themselves together, which is curious in view of the fact that the statue itself is shown stepping out of broken shackles.

One Mother's Day weekend two men scaled the outside of the statue in mountaineer fashion. Using rubber suction cups they reached a spot midway between the statue's shoulder blades, secured themselves, and there they hung. They unrolled a banner protesting an FBI action, recited poetry, and let themselves down the next morning to be arrested.

Dave Moffitt, the superintendent who proudly cares for the lady of the harbor.

101

A Permit, Please

Dave Moffitt has no problem with demonstrators if they follow the rules. "The statue is the most appropriate place in America to demonstrate," he says, "but please get a permit." When telephoned in advance, his staff will provide bleachers, bullhorns, and a nice spot by the flagpole.

"But naturally," he adds wearily, "an illegal act gets more attention."

In 1980 someone exploded a bomb in the base of Miss Liberty. No one was hurt nor was the statue damaged.

Five and a half hours after the bombing, eleven phone calls claiming responsibility were received by the FBI and New York *Times.* Three from the anti-Castro Omega-7, four from the Nationalist Socialist Movement, two from Puerto Rican FALN, one

Unveiling of the statue on October 28, 1886.

from the Palestine Liberation Army, and one (denied later) from the Jewish Defense League.

The group most suspected, the Croatian "freedom fighters," did not call.

"I can understand demonstrations of all kinds," says Dave Moffitt. "I can understand the twisted logic of, but not condone, the bombing of symbols of oppression, 'evil' government, and repression. But why would anyone want to destroy freedom?"

There is no law protecting Miss Liberty's employment in advertising and other commercial ventures as there is with the American flag. Thus she has been portrayed wearing everything from cowboy boots (to promote a radio station) to sun glasses, fur coats, plus holding up cans of cola.

A Human Fly

"I believe this sort of thing is self-defeating," says Moffitt. "It seems to incur the ire of people instead of making them likely customers for the product involved. One day a yogurt company wanted to film a television commercial of a man, who was a human fly, perched on the statue's head while eating their yogurt. We wouldn't allow it for safety reasons, and they countered with the argument that they could arrange the same scene using trick photography. I said, 'Sure, you can, but you'll end up the loser.' I showed them a sheaf of letters from people all over the country, many of them school children, who have written us expressing their disgust at seeing the statue commercialized. The yogurt company saw the light and ended up filming the human fly eating his snack on top of a Manhattan skyscraper."

Despite the advertising, the demonstrations, and the few attempts to destroy her, Miss Liberty remains solid, steady, and unharmed. Does she enjoy some kind of spiritual protection?

The Black Tom Explosion

She has already withstood one of the largest explosions in history. In August 1916 German saboteurs blew up a giant munitions plant on Black Tom Island, part of Jersey City, only a half-mile away. Yet, thanks to Miss Liberty's strong underpinnings and ingenious design, she was not seriously harmed by the tremendous force of the blast.

Many people believe that it was something far deeper than love of freedom in the souls of Laboulaye and Bartholdi, both deeply religious men, that inspired them to create this statue. And what about the others? Pulitzer who fought so hard for fairness and equality? And Emma Lazarus who, not until she felt a "religious fervor," gave Miss Liberty a soul?

There is no doubt in the minds of many that she has a spiritual heritage. And, if so, does she not symbolize the hopes of our people, our foundation of freedom, our deep-rooted faith?

Charlie DeLeo, a young man who works at the statue, believes that she does. And because of this he prays regularly for America in one of the most unusual "chapels" that has ever existed.

Charlie DeLeo fell in love with the Statue of Liberty in 1957 when he was nine years old. And, because of that, he probably has the most unique relationship with Miss Liberty of any person today.

He first met her when his fourth-grade teacher took his class of Lower East Side youngsters on a ferry ride to visit the statue. He was spellbound by the 305-foot structure, giddy over the adventure of climbing the narrow fifteen-story circular staircase to the crown. Children's voices piped out the 171 steps aloud as they made their ascent. Then, a little fearful, his class gathered in front of the twenty five windows in her diadem and stared down at the toy-like ships in the harbor.

Charlie felt a small shiver during that moment. It was the beginning of a beautiful, mystical relationship. His teacher explained that the gigantic woman, a gift of friendship from the people of France, symbolized much of what Americans hold dear—the active pursuit of freedom, a generous spirit, and the welcoming of all people regardless of their backgrounds or circumstances.

As he grew older, he visited Miss Liberty on his own. He was struck by the expression of strength and courage sculpted into her features. Later he would realize the enormity of those features— eyes two and one-half feet wide, a nose four and one-half feet long, and a three-foot-wide mouth.

12 ★

KEEPER OF THE FLAME

For a Special Reason

In his late teens he left his home and New York to go to Vietnam to fight. While there, he survived six mortar attacks and saw the suffering and horrible deaths that men were inflicting on one another. He also developed a deeper relationship with God and came to the realization that not killing, but caring for life, should be our purpose. He felt, too, that God had protected him during the war for some special reason; but when he returned home in 1969 and went aimlessly from one job to the next, he couldn't discover why.

On a brisk spring day in 1972, he took the $1.50 round-trip ferry ride out to Liberty Island* to collect his thoughts. When he stepped off the boat, he responded to an urging that he felt on the way over. The thought had never occurred to him before. But there it was, a very insistent voice within him which he believes was the Holy Spirit: *Ask for a job here!* So he stepped into the office

*In 1956, a Congressional resolution changed the name from Bedloe's to Liberty Island, the name Bartholdi had called it all along.

and did just that, and he was hired on the spot.

A Spirit of Caring

As a member of the maintenance crew, he scraped and painted Liberty's spiral staircases, cleaned her windows, replaced them with screens for the warm months, and swept her paths. Here at last he was *caring for something;* and day by day he learned more about the great national monument.

He learned all he could about her creation, about Laboulaye, Bartholdi, and the others, how she was constructed. He particularly took note of her design—the broken shackles representing triumph over tyranny and the seven rays on her crown symbolizing liberty radiating to the seven continents and seven seas.

But it was the torch that she held in her right hand that fascinated him. The ladder to the torch was off limits and has been forbidden to tourists since 1916. Rumor has it that a weakness in her arm made it unsafe. But that is not the case. It is just that the tiny ladder cannot accommodate the one and a half million tourists that now visit the statue each year.

Charlie DeLeo, keeper of the flame.

On the Torch

One day shortly after he began working at the statue, Charlie DeLeo unlocked the metal gate leading to her right arm. And he slowly climbed the forty-two-foot narrow ladder leading up through Miss Liberty's arm. The ladder, only twelve inches wide, ended at a trapdoor. He put his shoulder to the hatch, it creaked open, and he stepped onto the open catwalk encircling the torch. He found himself facing the most glorious view of the New Jersey flatlands, Brooklyn docks, and Manhattan skyscrapers.

There he was, standing alongside the torch, its 200 panes of amber glass which sent out a 2000-watt beacon from the four high-intensity sodium vapor lamps within. He was so drawn to this lofty hideaway with its bird's-eye view of God's world that he often took his lunch up there.

Perched above her eight-foot-long fingers, sitting in the open air on the torch catwalk thirty stories above the harbor, he could feel the torch sway in the brisk harbor breezes and yet felt secure, secure in the hand of Liberty. He thought of all those people, the "huddled masses yearning to breathe free" that Emma Lazarus spoke of in her poem on the statue's base. He thought of his grandparents who were among those standing at a ship's rail, straining to catch the first glimpse of this symbol of hope for *all* peoples.

However, one day his supervisor learned of his frequent trips to the torch and called him into his office. Charlie felt sure that he was going to be reprimanded because the right arm and torch were off limits. He stood in front of the supervisor's desk, apprehensive, waiting.

"DeLeo," said the supervisor, "I hear you've been climbing the stairwell to the torch..."

"Yes, well," mumbled Charlie. "I have gone up there..." He shuffled from one foot to the other, awkwardly.

Charlie DeLeo at work in his lofty "office."

Keeping the Flame

"Well," said the supervisor, "since you're spending so much time up there, I thought we'd just put you in charge of it. You'll have to keep the glass cleaned, maintain the area, and see to it that the flame is always burning. What do you say?"

Charlie was astounded. He was being assigned to maintain what he considered the most significant part of the statue—the beacon of freedom to all people!

"Sure, I'll do it!" he yelled happily.

So that is why today Charlie DeLeo is known as the Keeper of the Flame. Before the statue's renovations, he climbed up there twice a week to check the lamps and polish the panes so that the rays of light would continue to reach as far as possible. He thinks of this flame as representing the people of America whenever he reads that passage in Matthew that says: "You are the light of the world....Let your light so shine before men, that they may see your good works and glorify your Father in heaven" (5:14, 16).

Men, women, and children all over the country have learned about Charlie DeLeo from newspaper and magazine articles and television programs. Many write him and he treasures the letters, including one from the president of the United States.

Charlie answers his letters, as many as he can. And often he will enclose copies of the poems he has written about liberty and freedom, poems that he feels are inspired by the Holy Spirit.

School children have become pen pals with Charlie DeLeo; he always sends them a personal reply along with information on the Statue of Liberty, always ending his letters with a "God bless you."

He feels especially close to God up there by the torch where one day, overcome by the power of the Holy Spirit, he began praising God and singing hymns. Then he knelt and dedicated his life to the service of Jesus Christ; "My Savior was now my Lord," he says.

An Unusual Chapel

And that is why he has come to regard the torch as a chapel. Often on his daily rounds he will climb to it. The afternoon sun is high as he looks out over the railing—out to the sea and the lands beyond, then over to the mainland with its factories and homes and office buildings. He thinks beyond to the suburbs and farms and to the cities and villages beyond them to all parts of America. And he thinks of all the people out there who make up our great land.

Then, as he always does when he is in Liberty's "chapel," he kneels and prays for all Americans. He prays that we will enjoy the fullness of life in the spirit of liberty; that we will cling to those ideals that have made our country a beacon around the world; and that every man, woman, and child will come to know life, liberty, and the pursuit of happiness that God intended for us all.

*"An American Beauty" by Charles DeLeo, adapted with permission from *Guideposts* magazine. Copyright © 1982 by Guideposts Associates, Inc., Carmel, N.Y. 10512. All rights reserved.

13
SAVING THE LADY

"Where moth and rust destroy..." were Jesus' words on the perishability of all earthly material (Matt. 6:19). And the Statue of Liberty is no exception.

Not long after her dedication her new penny-bright exterior took on the moss green patina that all exposed copper develops, which protects it from further corrosion.

Other than that, she has weathered the years quite well. However, by her ninetieth birthday it was easy to see by those who knew her intimately that man and weather had taken their toll. In fact, she was in mortal danger.

Water seeping through cracks and crevices had greatly weakened her structurally. "One morning we found a small piece of her crown lying on the ground at the base," said David Moffitt. "It probably had fallen during the night."

Much of the problem was caused by man. When the three hundred copper sections were reassembled in New York in 1886, they did not fit together as well as they did in Paris. Some felt this was due to the tremendous New York summer heat which expanded the copper.

The Hole in Her Arm

To accommodate the changes, workmen often had to drill new rows of rivet holes. When Miss Liberty's head was finally secured in place, it was two feet off the center line. The torch-bearing arm was one and a half feet out of plumb. As a result one spike in the crown began rubbing against the arm as it swayed in the wind, and after a number of years a hole was worn in the arm.

Another opening into which rain found its way was the torch itself. Originally, it was constructed as a solid flame. But holes were cut into it later to allow light to shine out. Water leaking through these holes damaged the torch and arm frame.

Further corrosion damage was caused by the electrolysis action where the iron support bars met the copper skin. Bartholdi had tried to prevent this by affixing pads between the copper and iron, but in time these disintegrated.

A Strange Story

Repairs, in fact, have been made from time to time throughout the years. And one of the most fascinating occasions, because of its unique historical sidelight, was handled by Kenneth Lynch, Sr., now of Wilton, Connecticut.

Kenneth Lynch had a deep feeling for the statue ever since his father took him to visit it in 1912 when he was a youngster. He revisited it from time to time, and in 1927 while there, he learned it was in need of repairs. As a seasoned blacksmith and metal craftsman, he was offered the job.

Very familiar with the *repoussé* method of forming copper sheeting into desired shape, he knew that proper working of copper demanded specially designed tools, some of which he owned. Planning to make do with what he had, he returned to the Statue of Liberty and made an unexpected, but happy, find. Deep in the statue's basement he came across some dusty wooden packing crates shipped over with the statue in 1885. Curious, he dug into them and found a treasure: over thirty-five *repoussé* tools, hammers, stakes, wedges, and mallets. They had obviously been used by the Parisian workers in crafting the 300 copper plates of the statue.

With these and his own tools, Kenneth Lynch happily set to work on the demanding and intricate task of reshaping and replacing copper sections and replacing rivets. Because of inclement weather, it took him a year and a half. Without the fortunate find of the tools, it would have taken him much longer.

Kenneth Lynch enjoyed a special satisfaction in working with those old French tools. In a way, he felt them hallowed, considering they had been used to build the statue he had come to love and respect.

When his work was completed, he tried to return the tools to the officer in charge of the statue, pointing out their value and suggesting that they be placed in a museum. To his surprise he was rebuffed. The officer declared that his work contract stipulated that Lynch had to leave the premises "broom clean" and that meant not leaving any tools behind.

Reluctantly, Lynch took them home and for over fifty years made special efforts to donate them not only to the Statue of Liberty but to various government historical museums around the nation. None of them wanted the tools that made the statue.

He could have easily sold them through antique galleries for a tremendous sum. One collector offered him eight thousand dollars for the set. But Kenneth Lynch felt that the historical artifacts belonged to the people of the United States, and he determined that someday they would be returned to their proper home.

Finally, in 1982 his efforts succeeded when the tools were welcomed home by David Moffitt, superintendent of the Statue of Liberty. In appreciation of his efforts, Kenneth Lynch was "given" the Statue of Liberty for one day, April 3, 1982. It was an especially meaningful day for the metal craftsman, and he invited five hundred of his friends to share it with him.

Kenneth Lynch stills run his metal-crafting firm, Kenneth Lynch & Son, in Wilton, Connecticut. Renowned for their metal artistry, his craftsmen have made everything from suits of armor to ornamental iron work and artistic statuary.

Today the tools that were used in building the Statue of Liberty are on display, along with the story of the man who saved them, in the Story Room museum inside the statue's base. The Story Room at the statue and its related American Museum of Immigration are open to tourists seven days a week.

Another popular attraction on Liberty Island is the gift shop and restaurant.

What Souvenirs Do Visitors Buy Most?

Reproductions of Miss Liberty. These range in size from three-fourths-inch-high charms for bracelets, which cost from $4.00 to $380 depending on their material, to an eight-foot-high model of the statue molded of fiberglass with a $900 price tag.

Jim Hill, president of the E. Hill Group, a family owned and operated enterprise which has been serving Liberty Island visitors for over a half-century, says the giant-size figure is usually purchased by those using it for promotional purposes such as film companies.

The most popular model of the statue is 9 1/4 inches tall, of Flemish metal, which sells for $5.45. Hill pointed to a six-inch-high "not-for-sale" model on display which is actually a historical artifact. It is one of the last remaining samples of the model that was sold at the statue at the turn of the century. "The fact that it sold for one dollar compared to similar ones today going for only twice the price is a tribute to modern mass-production techniques," says Hill.

The Hills confine their gift-shop merchandise to items that have a direct relationship to the statue. These range from glassware with Miss Liberty in molded relief to a wide collection of books on the statue and nearby Ellis Island. The firm designs much of its own merchandise using its own dies, molds, and art concepts. The firm steers clear of the gaudy and sensational. "Sticking a souvenir decal on a Frisbee doesn't make it an item for us," says Hill. Through the years various companies have tried, without success, to press an assortment of fad items onto their shelves.

"We know these items will sell," shrugs Hill, "but not only would they conflict with our policy of staying away from gimmick items, they would also put us in a poor light with our landlord, Uncle Sam. The more we stay in line with his desire to see tasteful and meaningful gifts on display, the better our business seems to be," continued Hill, "and that says something about our landlord's policies."

The Hill family must be doing many things right for they have been Liberty Island's only gift shop tenant since founder Aaron Hill, Jim's father, first opened a small gift counter on the visitors' pier in 1931.

"Dad was an army veteran," says Jim, who was born on the island in 1925 and is a World War II Air Corps veteran himself. "Dad served in the Mexican Border War and, after his discharge in 1929, worked as a civilian at Fort Wood's post exchange on the island when it was still an army installation.

"His forefathers, Scottish and Irish, settled in America in the early 1800s, but my mother who helped in the shop with Dad came over here as a young girl from Poland. She has a special feeling for Miss Liberty, having first seen her from the deck of her incoming ship."

Founder Aaron Hill died in 1943, but his wife, Evelyn, (the "E" in the firm's name) still comes out to the island often to see how her family is getting along. Jim's son, Brad, also works in the family business which now employs some sixty people. Its clientele has included practically every U.S. president since Grover Cleveland.

The Hills have seen gift buying habits shift through the years. "Chinaware is more in demand now," says Jim, "and we notice that ash trays and cigarette lighters have slumped in popularity, reflecting increasing public awareness of the dangers of smoking."

Interestingly, foreign visitors buy more gifts than Americans. "The German and Japanese tourists are among the biggest spenders," said Hill, "concentrating on small items which can be easily packed."

The Hills also feed the hungry on Liberty Island in their cafeteria. The most popular food items? What else but the all-American favorites—hamburgers and fried chicken.

Never Intended for Tourists

Actually, the Lady on Liberty Island was never intended to host tourists. The 171-step spiral staircase within her was to be only for

maintenance men. But who could deny all those who wanted to climb to her brow from the start? By 1983 a daily average of twenty-five hundred people was clambering the narrow walkway to Liberty's crown.

"In the summer, heat inside the statue is suffocating, especially during peak hours," read the report by the consulting architects of Swanke Hayden Connell of New York. "Humidity is often unbearable, and carbon dioxide levels exceed acceptable limits. In the winter the interior is heated by radiators. The natural draft of air flow from the bottom of the interior of the statue to the top is the only ventilation."

Obviously, tourists' comfort leaves much to be desired. Few real improvements have been made on the statue since its dedication, and those that were made were mainly exterior.

Take her lighting, for example.

"The Lighthouse"

Since Miss Liberty was originally considered a beacon for mariners, Congress placed her in care of the Federal Lighthouse Board. At this time circular holes—almost a foot in diameter—were cut out of the solid torch to allow light to show from within. This was a failure; even Bartholdi complained that from a distance it "looked like a glowworm."

In 1892 the Lighthouse Board in a "Notice to Mariners" announced that a vertical beam of red and yellow light would shine from the torch while "the face and bust...will be illuminated by a powerful search light."

Still, this did not offer enough illumination to be a proper lighthouse and our government finally gave up the endeavor, transferring it in 1902 to the War Department. In 1933 it was taken over by its most logical guardian, the National Park Service.

An endeavor to floodlight the entire statue at night began in 1916 when war clouds darkened Europe. The New York *World* again launched a fund-raising campaign and again the people responded. Part of the $30,000 collected went to refashion Liberty's torch. Gutzon Borglum, who later became famous for his Mt. Rushmore faces, cut 600 large pieces out of it, replacing them with amber-colored cathedral glass.

This is when the rain began to really drain into the torch.

The remainder of the money was spent on floodlighting. That, however, created unpleasant shadows across Miss Liberty's face, and in 1931 a more powerful and improved system was installed.

In 1976, in time for our nation's bicentennial, even stronger lighting flooded Miss Liberty, giving her a beacon power that Bartholdi probably had in mind when he designed her.

While much attention was being focused on her exterior, her interior remained in the dark as far as real preventative maintenance was concerned. In 1982 a team of French and American architects, concerned about her interior, examined Miss Liberty minutely and pinpointed a host of trouble spots. They estimated restoration of the statue would amount to $20 to $30 million, some sixty times its original cost.

A committee of concerned men and women was formed and it was decided that an overall financial goal of $230 million would be needed, not only to restore the statue and its neighboring historical landmark, Ellis Island, but to provide endowment funds for future maintenance, plus an educational program, centennial celebrations, and administrative costs.

The funds are being collected by the Statue of Liberty–Ellis Island Foundation which is chaired by Lee Iacocca, Chairman of Chrysler Corporation. Work on the statue is being done under the direction of the American architectural firm of Swanke Hayden Connell in association with architect Thierry Despont.

When the restoration is completed, tourists will find:

- a completely new torch which will duplicate the original one. To be solid copper, gold-gilded, it will be powerfully floodlighted. Ten French copper workers fashioned the new torch using the historic *repoussé* method while working in a shop on the island for the benefit of visitors. The old, fragile, glazed torch will be placed on exhibit in the museum at the statue's base.
- a new viewing platform within Miss Liberty's brow.
- an improved spiral staircase, with additional resting platforms, from which climbers can see the magnificent interior of the statue.
- all new strapwork supporting the copper skin, using modern stainless steel alloys to replace the 1,350 old iron bars.
- new copper plates, where needed, including some 20,000–25,000 copper rivets.
- a strengthened right arm.
- General Electric has designed new metal halide lighting fixtures (each light equals one million candlepower) to floodlight the statue without shadows.
- a new larger, double-decked hydraulic glass-enclosed elevator within the pedestal will replace the existing one, which car-

ries visitors from ground level to the colonnade level. It will also accommodate disabled tourists. It will be the tallest hydraulic elevator in the country.

- a special mini-elevator to the statue's shoulder for emergency use.
- closed-circuit TV cameras affording views from within and outside of the statue at various levels for those who do not wish to ascend to the top.
- greater comfort from an improved air circulation system which will help maintain proper air quality.
- a new view of the vast proportions of the pedestal's vaulted interior, previously obstructed by unnecessary platforms.
- an open-air balcony midway up the base at the colonnade level will be opened to the public.
- the exterior will be washed with detergent, but its protective green copper oxide patina will remain intact.
- a special vantage point in the mezzanine level allowing visitors to peer up into the statue's mammoth interior, which will be cleaned of its old green paint and tar, allowing the brown patina of the copper to show. Removing the seven layers of paint will be accomplished by spraying it with supercold liquid nitrogen (-350F) which will freeze the paint, causing it to drop off in small flakes. Coarse-grained bicarbonate of soda will then be used to blast off the old tar.

What about the misalignment of Miss Liberty's head and arm? It will not be touched; the architects feel this is too unnoticeable to make any difference.

In January 1984 aluminum scaffolding began to be unloaded on Liberty Island to enclose the statue in a gigantic "cage" from which craftsmen will work. Miss Liberty herself may be closed to visitors for as long as a year while interior work is underway, but Liberty Island will remain open during the entire restoration period.

The statue is now surrounded by scaffolding as renovation is underway.

Looking Her in the Eye

The workmen, together representing about as many ethnic groups as the statue has welcomed to America, refer to her as "the Lady." As reported by the New York *Times,*[1] each of them feels there is something special about his job. Bob Conmy, who was on the crew that built the scaffolding surrounding the statue, was

[1]William E. Geist, "Special Feelings About Work on a Special Statue," New York *Times,* June 30, 1984, sec. B.

one of the first people in 198 years to look her right in the two-and-a-half-foot eye. He gave her a kiss...

Angelo Bommarito, labor foreman on the project, immigrated from Italy eighteen years ago at the age of seventeen. He tells of his arrival on a ship from Italy at 3:00 A.M. and of seeing the Statue of Liberty for the first time. "I cannot talk about my feelings," he said. "To me, the job is a little special. I come from the other side..."

Paul Gabriel, a forty-five-year-old electrician from New Jersey, said he has become an important person to family and friends. "I have worked on a lot of jobs, including the World Trade Center. Working on the Lady here, you realize that the trade center was just a tall building." Tom Snodgrass, supervisor of the project for the general contractors, Lehrer/McGovern, Inc., has a reputation among the men for toughness. He talked of arriving on the island

at 6:30 A.M. before any of the other workers. "It's very quiet," he said. "You can take the time to notice little things about her, the little creases in her hands, the spots on her arms and little welts in her throat that need to be tended to. She's a different color in the morning light. It's quite a sensation to touch her face. Very few people have done that."

Joe Fiebiger works inside the statue making molds of each one of the 1,200 corroded armatures that attach the superstructure of the statue to the copper skin and hold its shape. Each one must be replaced. Each is different, following the contour of the flow of the robe, the slant of the nose and the like.

"I guess," said Fiebiger, "whether we admit it or not, we're all in love with her, for different reasons. I don't want to sound foolish. I'm a blacksmith."[2]

A Great Day

The work, along with collecting the $230 million needed to accomplish it, plus the Ellis Island renovation, is expected to be completed in time for the one hundredth anniversary of the statue's dedication, October 28, 1986. On July 4th, 1986, the restoration will be celebrated as the focal point of Liberty Centennial Week involving a huge flotilla of The Tall Ships in New York harbor, the world's largest fireworks display, and July 4th parades throughout America.

Thousands of business corporations and individuals have already contributed money, including Kathleen Corkery of Elmhurst, New York, who wrote: "I came here from Ireland in 1948; my husband in 1949. We love this wonderful country. God bless and protect her and guide her for all our children to enjoy the peace we enjoy."

Shirley Gottlieb Bier of Brooklyn in sending her donation said: "When something special occurs for me or my family [such as one of her grandchildren being ordained a rabbi or a son graduating from medical school], I look to the heavens and say, 'Sophie Gottlieb [her mother], look how far we have come from the ghettos of Poland.' "

Again, the Children

And again, America's children are expected to play a large part in this campaign. Using the statue and Ellis Island as symbols, the

[2]Ibid., sec. B.

Liberty Centennial Student Campaign will focus on developing among the young a greater understanding of the role of immigration and ethnic diversity in our nation's history. It will also seek to instill a greater appreciation of freedom and liberty as enduring national values.

The campaign began bearing fruit early in 1983 when 24,200 Bridgeport, Connecticut children, in both public and parochial schools, collected $3,587 to help restore the statue.

When six-year-old Michael Haverly of Shelbyville, Indiana, a boy with crippled hands and arms, heard a committee was trying to raise money to repair the statue, he decided to launch a fund drive of his own. The kindergarten pupil at Triton Elementary School had raised sixty-seven dollars by 1984, thanks to the help of a very extended family. Michael is the adopted son of parents who have made a vocation of taking in foster children with special needs. There are five other children, and the Haverlys have cared for 150 foster children. Michael said he wanted to help save the statue "because my mom told me it stands for liberty and justice for all. The next thing my mom told me is, it's a symbol for the country. I keep that in mind."

"It snowballed," recalled his mother, Connie Haverly. "It became his personal business."

Michael found a plastic bucket, festooned it with photographs and his own drawing of the Statue of Liberty, and took it to a Parent-Teacher organization meeting.

"He went around from person to person. It would just make you choke up to see those little arms around that bucket," his mother said. "People would listen to his spiel and dig in. He got ten dollars that night."

From there Michael moved to his school, where Principal David Sever let him make his pitch over the intercom. "I was shaking in my bones," Michael said. "But I knew what I had to say, and I knew how to say it."

It is easy to see from the spirits expressed above that the campaign will more than achieve its goal.

Donations may be mailed to:

THE STATUE OF LIBERTY

and

ELLIS ISLAND FOUNDATION, INC.

P.O. Box 1986

New York, New York 10018

The pilgrims don't come by ship anymore...

As the jet airliner thundered toward New York, a young Cuban boy peered out his seat window anxiously watching for that special symbol he had heard so much about since childhood. It was a pleasant February afternoon in 1965. But five miles above the earth, teen-ager Dagoberto Jorge was apprehensive about what awaited him after his plane landed. He felt that just seeing that symbol would give him the confidence he so desperately needed.

But was it still there? The famous statue he had so often read and heard about that welcomed newcomers to the land of freedom? Some people in Cuba had told him she was gone. Oh yes, they grimaced, she still stood in the harbor somewhere but she didn't mean anything anymore.

"America doesn't want you," they said. "There is no real opportunity there anymore, only crime, racial strife, and much poverty. You'll come back soon, begging to be let in."

Sardonic comments had seemed the rule in his homeland ever since it fell into chaos in 1959. Businesses had been nationalized, free enterprise was banned, some churches were closed. Repression was so intense that few ventured to attend services at those remaining.

IS SHE STILL THERE?

Leaving Home

To Dagoberto freedom was a precious God-given gift. And if he couldn't have it at home, he vowed to go where it still existed. It took him three years and many little miracles to get his papers ready. Finally in 1964, with only a small suitcase holding a change of clothes, Dagoberto left his family and homeland behind as countless others from Europe had done a century earlier. His heart ached and his head was bent. But a promise sustained him, a verse he had marked in the Bible: "Stand fast therefore in the liberty by which Christ has made us free, and be not entangled again with a yoke of bondage" (Gal. 5:1).

He made his way to Mexico City, a first step in reaching his goal. There, after trying almost a year, he obtained his green card and went to Miami where he boarded a New York–bound plane.

A Mistake?

Now, as the plane neared its destination, fear gripped him. He did not speak English; he did not have one friend to turn to in that giant city. What if the others back home had been right about

Dagoberto at work today.

America? Had he made a terrible mistake? And that is why he so anxiously searched below for the Statue of Liberty. If he could just *see* it for himself. Then, somehow he would *know* that if she were still there, truly there, that America was all his early reading had promised.

Few new arrivals to America come by ship anymore. Instead, huge jets thunder into Kennedy and Newark International airports, and it's rare that passengers catch sight of the statue. But Dagoberto, scrunched close to his window port, watched. Suddenly, the pilot's voice sounded over the public-address system.

"We are fortunate to be over New York harbor, folks," he said. He pointed out that passengers on the right-hand side could get a good view of the Statue of Liberty. With face pressed to the glass and heart pounding, Dagoberto peered down at the harbor waters sparkling in the afternoon sun.

And there she was.

"She was just as I pictured her," he says, "even from above she looked so majestic standing there in the middle of the harbor. And," he added in awe, "she was raising her glowing torch to me! All of my doubts were washed away in seeing her. My heart lifted and tears filled my eyes as I knew deep within my heart that, yes, the Statue of Liberty was still there, truly there."

"I knew just what the other immigrants seeking freedom felt when they saw her for the first time from the decks of their ships," he said. "And I could feel the same infusion of strength and confidence that they were given."

A Vow to Contribute

Dagoberto Jorge stepped off that plane that February afternoon vowing to contribute to that American dream in every way possible.

He took any work he could, studied English at night, and learned different skills from typing to graphic arts, anything that might be of help to someone.

Some months later he heard that a magazine needed someone to run their auto-type machine for a week. It was *Guideposts*, an interfaith inspirational magazine that presents stories by people from all walks of life who tell how they have overcome problems and found new hope and courage through their faith in God. Dagoberto liked its philosophy and the way it seemed to help people. He also noted a formula for success that *Guideposts'* publisher, Norman Vincent Peale, often quoted: "Find a need and fill it." Dagoberto looked for needs to fill and worked so diligently that he was invited to join its staff. Today, eighteen years later in 1985, his name is listed on the magazine's masthead as Assistant Art Director.

Every so often Dagoberto takes the subway down to the tip of Manhattan Island where waves lap at the Battery and says a quiet hello "to the Lady."

"I look around and see people of all races," he says, "and I see God's promise of liberty in every face. It's a kind of light. I look out into the harbor and see that same light in the torch of the Statue of Liberty, and I realize that all of us, newcomers and generations-old citizens alike, have a holy responsibility to carry that light of tolerance and compassion with us wherever we go."

Skywriting above the statue.

Will we continue to become the country God had in mind when He first blessed us?

For some answers, we can go back fifty years to the golden anniversary of Miss Liberty when the thirty-second president of the United States, Franklin Delano Roosevelt, spoke at the October 28, 1936, ceremonies. Here are some excerpts from his speech:

> Four hundred years ago, in Europe as well as in Asia, there was little hope of liberty for the average man of courage and good will. The ambitions of a ruling class and the times alike conspired against liberty of conscience, liberty of speech, liberty of the person, liberty of economic opportunity. Wars...dynastic and religious, had exhausted both the substance and the tolerance of the Old World. There was neither economic nor political liberty—nor any hope for either.

> Then came one of the great ironies of history. Rulers needed to find gold to pay their armies and increase their power over the common man. The seamen they sent to find that gold found instead the way of escape for the common man from those rulers. What they found over the Western horizon was not the silk or jewels of Cathay, but mankind's second chance—a chance to create a new world after he had almost spoiled an old one.

> And the Almighty seems purposefully to have withheld that second chance until the time when men would most need and appreciate liberty, the time when men would be enlightened enough to establish it on foundations sound enough to maintain it. For over three centuries a steady stream of men, women, and children followed the beacon of liberty which this light symbolizes....

> They brought to us strength and moral fiber developed in a civilization centuries old but fired anew by the dream of a better life in America. They brought to one new country the cultures of a hundred old ones.

> ...They were men and women who had the supreme courage to strike out for themselves, to abandon language and relatives, to start at the bottom without influence, without money, and without knowledge of life in a very young civilization....

> Perhaps Providence did prepare this American continent to be a place of the second chance. Certainly, millions of men and women have made it that. They adopted this homeland because in this land they found a home in which the things they most desired could be theirs—freedom of opportunity, freedom of thought, freedom to worship God. Here they found life because here there was freedom to live.

> It is the memory of all these eager seeking millions that makes this one of America's places of great romance....

QUO VADIS LIBERTY?

...Even in times as troubled and uncertain as these, I still hold to the faith that a better civilization than any we have known is in store for America and by our example, perhaps, for the world. Here destiny seems to have taken a long look. Into this continental reservoir there has been poured untold and untapped wealth of human resources. Out of that reservoir, out of the melting pot, the rich promise has not run out. If we keep the faith for our day as those who came before us kept the faith for theirs, then you and I can smile with confidence into the future....

Liberty and peace are living things. In each generation, if they are to be maintained, they must be guarded and vitalized anew. We do only a small part of our duty to America when we glory in the great past. Patriotism that stops with that is a too-easy patriotism—a patriotism out of step with the patriots themselves. For each generation the more patriotic part is to carry forward American freedom and American peace by making them living facts in a living present.

To that we can, we do, rededicate ourselves.

As that president said, it all depends on how each of us faces our responsibility to God, our country, our families, ourselves.

1865 Edouard de Laboulaye first suggests the idea of the Statue of Liberty. American Civil War ends. Abraham Lincoln assassinated. William Booth founds the Salvation Army in England. Lewis Carroll's *Alice's Adventures in Wonderland*; Leo Tolstoy's *War and Peace*.

1870 Bartholdi's first Liberty model. Franco-Prussian War. Dogma of papal infallibility. Wagner's *Die Walkure*.

1871 Bartholdi's first trip to America for Liberty project. British Parliament legalizes labor unions. Luther Burbank first experiments with plant breeding and hybrids. The great Chicago fire kills 300 and leaves 90,000 homeless. Stanley finds Livingstone in central Africa. Verdi composes *Aida* in honor of the opening of Suez Canal.

1874 Union Franco-Américaine formed in France to bring the Statue of Liberty into being. First zoo in America opens in Philadelphia. First electric streetcar appears in New York City. Barbed wire invented by Joseph Glidden. Louis Tiffany begins making his artistic glassware.

1875 Union Franco-Américaine launches appeal for funds in French newspapers. Bartholdi's final model for Liberty. Electric dental drill patented by George Green, Michigan inventor. Andrew Carnegie builds first Bessemer steel-making factory. First Kentucky Derby held in Louisville; Aristides wins. Tolstoy's *Anna Karenina*; Bizet's *Carmen*. Bartholdi begins "Lion of Belfort," completed 1880.

1876 Liberty's torch and right hand exhibited in Philadelphia. Rutherford Hayes elected President of the United States. Telephone patented by Alexander Graham Bell. General George Custer and 264 troops massacred in the Battle of Little Bighorn. Tchaikovsky's *Swan Lake*; Brahms's *First Symphony*; Mark Twain's *The Adventures of Tom Sawyer*.

1877 U.S. Congress officially accepts the gift of Liberty. Copper wire invented, greatly facilitating electronic communications. Intercity phone service begins between Chicago and Milwaukee, and between Boston and Salem, Mass. A new soft drink called root beer is produced and sold by Charles Hires. The first All-

FREEDOM'S HOLY LIGHT HISTORICAL TIMELINE

England Lawn Tennis Championship is won by Spencer Gore at Wimbledon.

1878 Liberty's head exhibited at Paris Fair.

1879 Gustave Eiffel becomes Liberty's engineer. Edison invents the incandescent electric lamp.

1881 Levi Morton, U.S. minister to France, drives first ceremonial copper rivet in body of statue, in Paris. Richard Hunt chosen as architect for pedestal. First color photo developed by Frederick Ives. Red Cross organized by Clara Barton. Booker T. Washington founds Tuskegee Institute. President Garfield is assassinated and succeeded by Chester Arthur. Twain's *The Prince and the Pauper*.

1883 Laboulaye dies. Emma Lazarus writes her famous poem, *The New Colossus*. Ground broken for the pedestal, and Joseph Pulitzer launches his newspapers campaign to fund it. Brooklyn Bridge completed. Machine gun invented. Volcano on Krakatoa explodes, killing 36,419 and sending tidal waves around the world. Twain's *Life on the Mississippi*; Robert Louis Stevenson's *Treasure Island*; Howard Pyle's *The Merry Adventures of Robin Hood*; Nietzsche's *Thus Spake Zarathustra*.

1884 Statue of Liberty officially presented to the U.S. at Paris ceremony on July 4. Cornerstone for pedestal laid in New York. Grover Cleveland elected President. Linotype typesetting machine invented by Mergenthaler; first successful fountain pen by Waterman. First subway begins operating in London. First state-supported women's college chartered in Columbus, Mississippi. Twain's *The Adventures of Huckleberry Finn*.

1885 Statue of Liberty arrives in New York. Pedestal fund completed as *New York World* raises $100,000. Pasteur invents the rabies vaccine. British General Gordon massacred in Khartoum by the Mahdi, who takes control of the Sudan. Stevenson's *A Child's Garden of Verses*; Gilbert and Sullivan's *The Mikado*.

1886 Liberty is unveiled in New York Harbor. Haymarket Square bombing in Chicago. American Federation of Labor (A.F. of L.) founded; Samuel Gompers elected president. Apache Indian wars end in American southwest. Westinghouse builds America's first successful A.C. power plant in Buffalo, New York. Stevenson's

The Strange Case of Dr. Jekyll and Mr. Hyde and *Kidnapped;* Nietzsche's *Beyond Good and Evil*.

1903 Bronze tablet bearing Emma Lazarus's poem mounted in Liberty's base. Wright brothers launch world's first successful manned flight in powered airplane at Kitty Hawk, N.C. Jack London's *The Call of the Wild;* Victor Herbert's *Babes in Toyland*.

1916 Statue modernized and floodlit at night. Mexico's "Pancho" Villa leads guerrilla raids into Texas and New Mexico. Electric clock invented. Einstein introduces his general theory of relativity. First professional golf tournament held in Bronxville, N.Y. Norman Rockwell begins illustrating covers for the *Saturday Evening Post*. Woodrow Wilson re-elected President.

1924 Statue of Liberty declared a national monument. Calvin Coolidge elected President. J. Edgar Hoover heads FBI. Lenin dies, and Joseph Stalin begins power struggle to succeed him. First Winter Olympics held in Chamonix, France. Metro-Goldwyn-Mayer and Columbia Pictures film companies formed.

June 6, 1944 D-Day! Liberty's torch turned on again after being turned off during the war. Allied troops land on north coast of France.

BENEDICTION
by Norman Vincent Peale

Lead Us Out of Darkness

I love the story about the little girl named Carol who went with her father for a ferryboat ride in New York harbor. It was late afternoon as they watched the Statue of Liberty disappear into the fog and shadows of approaching dusk.

Later that night Carol tossed restlessly in her bed. The father sat down beside her. "What's the matter, honey?"

"Oh, Daddy," she replied, "I've been thinking about the lovely lady out there in the darkness all by herself. She needs someone to help her hold up her lamp in the dark."

I'm convinced that the great majority of Americans love our land and, like Carol, want to uphold the freedoms on which our nation was founded. But these freedoms are under attack.

What can we do? Since America was founded, we have been strengthened—probably even saved—by the prayers of our people. The selfless prayers of enough people can and will see our nation through its present difficulties.

Disturbed that our citizens were depending too little on God, hotel owner Conrad Hilton helped create a prayer over 30 years ago called "America on Its Knees." I feel it is as timely now as it was then.

Our Father in Heaven:

We pray that You save us from ourselves. The world that You have made for us, to live in peace, we have made into an armed camp. We live in fear of war to come.

We are afraid of "the terror that flies by night, and the arrow that flies by day, the pestilence that walks in darkness and the destruction that wastes at noon-day."

We have turned from You to go our selfish way. We have broken Your commandments and denied Your truth. We have left Your altars to serve the false gods of money and pleasure and power. Forgive us and help us.

Now, darkness gathers around us and we are confused in all our counsels. Losing faith in You, we lost faith in ourselves.

Inspire us with wisdom, all of us, of every color, race and creed, to use our wealth, our strength, to help our brother, instead of destroying him. Help us to do Your will as it is done in Heaven and to be worthy of Your promise of peace on earth. Fill us with new faith, new strength, and new courage, that we may win the battle for peace. Amen.